"I'm almost never at home"

"I'm incurably forgetful"

"I'm afraid I don't know anything about gardening"

"I guess I just have the touch of death for plants"

You'll never be able to use these or other excuses for not enjoying plants in your home after reading this book. Whatever your problem, you'll find your answer here.

It might be a plant that grows with almost no light. It might be a mechanical device that takes all the guesswork out of gardening. It might be learning not to talk to your plants but to listen to what they are telling you. It might be knowing how to avoid any or all of the dreaded 12 Gardening Pitfalls.

It's all here . . . waiting for you to turn the page . . . waiting to turn you into the startlingly successful gardener you never thought you could be.

THE POPULAR LIBRARY
GARDENING SERIES

NEVER-SAY-DIE
HOUSE PLANTS

The Popular Library Gardening Series
Elvin McDonald, General Editor

POPULAR LIBRARY • NEW YORK

CONTENTS

ABOUT THE AUTHOR

Elvin McDonald is Senior Editor and Garden Editor of *House Beautiful* and Editorial Consultant for *Popular Gardening Indoors*. Since founding the American Gloxinia and Gesneriad Society when he was 14 years old, his writings about plants have appeared in every major magazine and newspaper. Since publication of his first book, *Miniature Plants for Home and Greenhouse,* in 1962, he has authored more than 40 others, some of which include *The World Book of House Plants, Little Plants for Small Spaces, The House Plant Answer Book, House Plants to Grow If You Have No Sun, The Complete Book of Gardening Under Lights, Miniature Gardens, Container Gardening, Good Housekeeping Basic Gardening Techniques, Good Housekeeping Planning the Perfect Garden,* and the 16-volume *Good Housekeeping Illustrated Encyclopedia of Gardening*.

Elvin McDonald resides in New York City in a high-rise apartment which he shares with two other adults, his three children, two cats, a dog—and approximately 400 plants at last count.

Introduction: Only a Plastic Plant Is Impossible to Grow

My affair with house plants began when I was three years old. It was, as I recall it now in adult terms, a crisp, clear October day in western Oklahoma and my mother knew that a killing frost was on its way. As she picked the last of the green tomatoes to make picalilli relish, I wandered around the vegetable garden feeling sad that Jack Frost was about to ruin what had been my summer playground. Then I discovered a volunteer bean sprout and I asked my mother if I could grow it in the house. Although she generally encouraged me, this time she said no, beans were not house plants, and besides they couldn't be transplanted. Rebellion. Of course, I could transplant it to a tin can of soil and make it grow. Well, that is exactly what happened. That plant grew all winter in a sunny window, up one side, across the top, and back down the other.

The amazing thing about what happened with the bean plant that fall and winter is that while Mamma was right, plants are unpredictable. No gardener to the trowel born would ever think of transplanting a bean seedling or growing it indoors in winter. When Mamma saw that I was going to dig up the bean, she wisely chose to consider that I was defying nature and not her. Rather than ignore or scold me, she put down her work and took the time to show me how to transplant a seedling growing in the open garden to a container of soil. She then explained that if the transplant was to live, I would have to take the responsibility of watering it often enough so that the soil would be always moist and never so dry as to cause the leaves to wilt. I also remember quite clearly that she told me the best place in the house for the bean plant would be one of the south-facing windows in the kitchen where there was lots of sun.

From that point on, the seedling grew like Jack's beanstalk. Mamma and Daddy both took as much pleasure in it as I did. Although they were the progeny of generations of farm folk, neither of them had ever isolated a single plant and watched it develop. They thought only in terms of a row of tomatoes, a patch of corn, or several hundred acres of wheat. The bean gave them a new sense of what they were all about and it taught me the essentials of container gardening. No matter how much it rained or snowed outdoors, I still had to water the bean often enough to keep the soil moist. And I could see that the leaves wanted to be in the sun because the stems always reached toward the window, not into the room. Three-year-olds of my generation did not have a busy schedule of watching television and going to nursery school, so I

10

had plenty of time to take care of my bean plant. Only once, the week following Christmas, did I forget to water it and the leaves wilted. Within a few hours after I gave it a drink, most of the leaves had perked up, but a few days later I saw that some of the older ones were turning yellow and sickly looking, and some of the baby leaves had dried up. Daddy showed me how to cut off what seemed to be dead and explained that this was called pruning, the same thing he did in early spring to the fruit trees which grew in the orchard in front of our house. He also cautioned that if I forgot to water the bean again it might not recover.

The next house plant I grew was a pink-flowered *Oxalis crassipes,* given to me by my Great Aunt Eulice. By that time I was four years old and totally fascinated by all house plants and by anyone who grew them. The moment Aunt Eulice matter-of-factly unpotted her big oxalis, broke it in half, repotted both and gave me the larger of the two, she became my favorite aunt. Then I climbed between my parents in the front seat of our pickup truck and we began the two-hour trip home. It was unbearably hot and by the time we got home we were all wilted, especially the oxalis. I took a big drink of water, shared it with the oxalis, and soon its leaves perked up. By the next day the plant was once again covered by pink flowers. I consider it my first never-say-die house plant and the inspiration for this book some 34 years later.

Actually, that particular oxalis is an especially tough plant because it grows from a fleshy rhizome or tuber in the soil that stores up moisture. If you should forget to water it for six months, all the leaves will die, but within five days after you soak the soil with water you will see the sprouts of new green growth. In a month's time there will be pink flowers—provided you continue to add water

11

when the surface soil feels dry to the touch of your fingers. Directly behind me as I write I have a plant of the same oxalis growing six inches below two 40-watt fluorescents which are burned 16 hours out of every 24. For over a year that plant has been covered with pink flowers, day in and day out. I see by the label it has been renamed *Oxalis rubra,* but otherwise it is the same good-natured plant I adopted as a four-year-old.

Most of my books begin as magazine pieces, and this one is no exception. When it became apparent a few years ago that people in general, not gardeners alone, were growing house plants, Wallace Guenther, Editor in Chief of *House Beautiful,* asked me to develop a feature on 12 plants with a strong will to live. As is our usual procedure, Wally asked me to work out the graphics with Ruth Weil, the Editorial Director. I did a lot of research, drew up my list of a dozen tough house plants and presented it to Ruth. As we went over the names and I showed her pictures of the plants, I was at first amused, and then deeply troubled as over and over she repeated, "But I've already killed this one."

That conversation with Ruth marked the turning point in my career as a garden writer. For the first time in my life, I went back to my office and tore up the draft of my manuscript for the piece and started over. I realized that I had been writing for gardeners, but failing to communicate with people. I was taking too much for granted, all the while ignoring the basics that result in living, thriving plants. My parting retort to Ruth was, "Only a plastic plant is impossible to grow," and with that in mind, I rewrote the piece, determined never again to think of myself as a garden writer, but rather as a writer committed to communicating the joy of gardening to any person who reads me, excluding no one by withholding essential information.

This book contains what you need to know to be a successful indoor gardener, but, like a good cookbook, at first you have to follow the instructions explicitly. Later, with experience, you can break the rules or change the ingredients to suit yourself, but not before you have a basic understanding of what it takes to nurture a potted plant indoors.

Elvin McDonald
New York City
December 1975

1. Why Do You Want to Grow Plants?

If you have clearly fixed in your mind why you want to grow plants, you'll have better luck with them. My friend Mary Otto drew this to my attention when she said that a lot of her young friends seemed to be buying plants because it was the thing to do. We decided that buying all the plants in the world will not make you chic, with it, or trendy, but the instant you discover how good a growing plant can make you feel, you're on to a lifetime, any time, anywhere activity.

And no person need be the kiss of death to flora. Like so many things in life, this is all a matter of conditioning. Several years ago three friends and I went on a Saturday plant hunting expedition to a range consisting of several large commercial greenhouses. Jeannene Booher, a Seventh Avenue fashion designer who is usually the epitome of sophisticated reserve, raced up and down the aisles with total abandon as she picked plants for her apartment. She had confidence. The thought of failure with any one of the plants never entered her mind.

The second of my friends, Lawrence Power, who owns his own public relations firm in New York, dealt with the array of plants more methodically, but with no less enthusiasm. Each time the form or color of a plant appealed to him I could see his mind ticking off, "Where would this look beautiful in my apartment or the house in the country?" and second, "How much light, water and warmth—or coolness—does it need to thrive?"

You must understand, I really love plants and few things turn me on as much as seeing friends and family I love react similarly. Even now, several years later, tingles of pleasure race through my head and down my arms as I recall Jeannene and Larry in those greenhouses.

Now we come to my third friend on the expedition, Mary Jo Clayton, who is vice president of an advertising agency, and one of those natural writers who even talks good copy. She was lost as she wandered along the aisles, first picking up this plant, then another, but always putting them back, moving along uncertainly and empty-handed.

By the time Jeannene, Larry, and I had made our selections, the checkout area had enough plants to open a shop. Even the owner, who is a good friend and a dyed-in-the-wool gardener's gardener, was seen briefly with dollar signs in his eyes. But Mary Jo was left out. No plant had spoken to her even though she'd tried. With certain desperation and a trace of cynicism she turned to a bench of piggyback plants and said, "Alright, which one of you wants to die?" As we all laughed, she picked her victim, paid its price and walked out, carrying the plant with all the insecurities a parent feels carrying home the first-born child from the hospital nursery.

Being able to grow plants is no different than being able to cook or make music. Some people have natural aptitude and some don't. Long ago we discovered that the can't-make-water-boil crowd could successfully cook up a feast with a good cookbook in hand or classes in gourmet cooking. And the kids who cried at the keyboard searching for the elusive middle C could as adults discover they were mad for music and look forward to lessons and practice with the same giddy anticipation of a tropical vacation in the dead of winter. Well, gardening is a game anybody can play. Naturals like Jeannene Booher, Larry Power —and Elvin McDonald—can always polish their game by study and experience, but basically they don't need help.

For my Mary Jo Clayton, and all the other Mary Jo Claytons in the world who want to grow plants, I have written this book. It's all a matter of selecting the right plants to live with you. By the right plants, I mean kinds that have a strong will to live. The sort of plant that won't die the first, or even second or third, time you forget to give it a drink of water when it is thirsty. The sort of plant that hangs in there long enough to build your confidence. All you have to do is succeed with one plant and you will have broken the green-thumb curtain. Forget any past failures. In fact, forget every plant except the one you are going to succeed with. The moment you realize that you and your plant have got it together you will never forget. Never.

And do you know why those of us who are nuts about gardening never stop growing and looking for new plants to make friends with? Because every time a plant responds favorably to you, the miracle happens again. It's the same

Author

One way to propagate the piggyback plant or tolmiea is to tape or pin the base of a mature leaf with a baby plant sprouting on it in the surface of a small pot of moist soil drawn up alongside the parent. As soon as the new plant begins to grow rapidly, you will know it has roots and the parent stem can be clopped in two.

as eating good food when you're hungry, drinking good wine when you're thirsty, or making love with the right person.

P.S. Mary Jo's piggyback plant died. Why? It has an enormous thirst. When it gets dry the leaves and stems collapse as if they would never rise again. But they will if watered within a few hours. The first time this happens some of the older leaves will die or turn brown along the edges. If drought strikes too often the plant will soon have no more leaves to turn brown.

Piggyback plant also prefers a cool, moist atmosphere. How do I know that? Because at some time in the past I looked up piggyback plant in a book. The line said, "See *Tolmiea*." And under tolmiea (toll-MEE-uh) I discovered that this plant grows wild all along the cool, moist Pacific coast from Alaska to northern California. Please don't misunderstand, I'm not saying the piggyback isn't a good house plant. It can be, but you have to be prepared to grow it where hot, midday sun does not shine directly on the leaves and also where hot, dry drafts from the heating system do not blow on it. You also have to keep the soil moist all the time. And one other thing, piggyback is by nature not a long-lived plant. Even under ideal conditions you have to start young plants from the babies that grow on top of the old leaves. Eventually you pitch out the old plant and replace it with the young.

Sounds simple, doesn't it? The truth is, the culture for most house plants is simple if you fix in your mind from the outset the growing conditions needed by each plant. Initially you have to think about it, and maybe refer to notes you've taken from a good reference. Eventually the care of each plant will come to you by second nature, the same as a favorite recipe. The first time I followed Julia Child through lemon-butter sauce it was a production number. I got more sauce on the book than on the artichokes for which it was intended. Now it's a part of me. I can double the recipe or triple it without conscious thought. Caring for plants is the same. And if you understand the idea behind the recipe—or the guidelines someone has set down for a particular plant's needs—you can adapt or improvise to fit the situation.

P.P.S. Mary Jo's story does have a happy ending. Based on the premise that she couldn't go through life thinking of herself as a plant murderer, she kept trying. The turning point came when Mary Jo realized that her apartment had a climate. And that its climate was decidedly warm in winter, the atmosphere was as dry as the Mojave, and there was almost no direct sun coming through the windows. Now she could look in a house plant book and find

19

lists of plants suggested for low-light areas, and also kinds that don't mind a hot, dry atmosphere in winter. The list wasn't long, but at least she could go to a shop and with some authority ask to see Chinese evergreen, *Dracaena fragrans* and Warneckei, sansevieria, pothos, heart- and fiddleleaf philodendron and Trileaf Wonder.

What happened at the shop is that Mary Jo decided a maranta or prayer plant was what she liked most. So she looked it up in a book and found that her climate was apparently to its liking, except for the dry atmosphere. She bought the maranta and set its pot in a north window on the surface of a tray of pebbles which she keeps wet. The last report is that Mary Jo called to say, "I've taken the plunge and divided my prayer plant." Feeling just a trace of giddiness at success, she kept the larger of the two just to be sure she didn't make her first plant friend feel unwelcome. She gave the smaller one, which had four leaves, to a human friend who was just getting started with plants. "Now it has 10 leaves and mine has 31. I'm still a leaf counter." We decided to meet for a celebration lunch and I could see that Mary Jo's right thumb was definitely turning green, "not emerald like yours, but at least it's chartreuse."

The most important thing Mary Jo did was to stop trying to grow plants blindly. Instead she thoughtfully evaluated the conditions of light, temperature, and humidity in her apartment. Of the three, light is the most difficult to judge, but to really succeed with plants you have to know what is going on in all departments.

2. The Facts of Light for House Plants

A few months ago I gave a lecture in the newly installed house plant shop on the main floor of a Chicago department store. While I was waiting to go on, I eavesdropped on conversations between the clerks and customers. Most of the advice I heard was not quite true and, sad to say, I am afraid this situation is more the rule than the exception. There seems to be a shortage of clerks who are actually plant people, not to mention the problem of semantics. For example, "This plant will grow well in your dark apartment because it doesn't need light." Anybody who sells plants should know that all house plants need light. The truth intended was that the plant in question did not need sun shining directly on its leaves.

There is of course a big difference between no light, light, and sun. If you do any photography, the differences between various amounts and sources of light will be obvious to you. To be a good indoor gardener, you really have to figure out how much light and how much sun shines into your apartment or office. Interestingly enough, most of us never think about this until we want to grow plants.

Unless trees, shrubs or other buildings prevent natural light from entering your windows, you will have bright light but no direct sun in a north window, a short half-day of direct sun in an east- or west-facing window, and a long half-day of direct sun in a south-facing window.

You can grow plants in any window through which enough light enters for you to read or do handwork by. North windows are not, of course, the only exposures without direct sun. A tall building, trees, or shrubs, may prevent direct sun from shining into an east, south, or west window. The south-facing windows of my apartment are more like east windows since a tall building across the street blocks out direct sun around 1 o'clock in the afternoon. I wasn't aware of this until I had lived in this apartment for a few months and had had the opportunity to be at home all day on several occasions. Then, as I puttered among my plants at different times of the day, I began to get a realistic picture of the amount of direct sun and bright light they were receiving.

The window in my dining room makes a good example of the various kinds of sun and light which may be found in and around almost any sunny window. Mine faces south and any plant placed directly in the window would receive a long half-day of direct sun if the long shadow of the building across the street did not cut it short. Even so, I find that almost all plants will grow in this kind of sun and light combination, cacti and other succulents included. However, tall plants placed on either side of the window

The highrise office of Lawrence Power, a partner of Power/ McGrath Associates, a public relations firm in New York City, faces west. The collection of plants, which receives full sun in the afternoon, includes (from left to right) a Dracaena marginata, *several Boston ferns, a grape-ivy, more Boston ferns and a* Monstera deliciosa *(a close relative of philodendron).*

next to the interior walls receive little or no direct sun, only bright light. By the same token, small plants placed on the floor under the window receive only bright light, no direct sun.

What all of this means is that by studying the sun and light patterns in this one window, I have been able to fill and surround it with plants, all of which thrive. The key to my success is that I have placed shade-loving plants where they will receive light but little or no direct sun, and have placed the sun-lovers where they receive the maximum amount of direct sun. As I write at the dining room table, the plants I see in the window are arranged as follows: to the left, with little or no direct sun, I have a 12-inch

"Silver King" aglaonema (Chinese evergreen) on the floor, with a slightly taller, flowering spathiphyllum and a silver-leaved rex begonia displayed in a pedestal. Also to the left of the window, and trained up the wall by means of masking tape to hold it in place is a red-leaved hybrid climbing philodendron with a hanging basket of hemigraphis (red ivy) meeting it in mid-air. To the right side of the window I have a grouping of three dracaenas (*Dracaena fragrans,* chartreuse-and-green-striped *D. fragrans massangeana,* and green-and-silver-variegated *D. goldieana*); on a good day these receive brief periods of direct sun, for up to an hour.

Directly on the sill, where they receive several hours of direct sun on a clear day, is an angraecum orchid, two pots of sweet basil which provide a constant and frequently used source of fresh seasoning, a flowering "Cloth of Gold" fancyleaf geranium, the perfect green-rose formation of an echeveria (a succulent), *Primula kewensis* with buds (this is a yellow-flowered primrose), a pair of compact coleus, a budded/miniature broughtonia orchid, a bromeliad— and a sprouted avocado pit. A huge plectranthus (Swedish ivy) which recently provided over 100 tip cuttings for my daughter Jeannene's classroom hangs from the ceiling directly in the center of the window where it receives maximum sun. And I have forgotten to mention that on the center of the dining table where I am writing there is a pottery container filled with thriving yellow-and-green-variegated scindapsus (pothos). This is seven feet back from the window, where the light is bright enough to comfortably read by in the daytime, and where at night it receives six to eight hours of supplementary illumination from a 100-watt spotlight in the ceiling fixture which is approximately six feet from the leaves.

If you want to grow plants, there is no such thing as an apartment with too much direct sun. You can always move shade-loving plants away from the sun, but if there is no

My collection of dracaenas thrives just to the right of the sunny south window in the dining room. They receive up to two hours of direct sun, but mostly bright light the rest of the day. They are (from left to right), D. marginata, D. fragrans massangeana, D. goldieana *(short plant in foreground with fancy leaves).* D. fragrans *(tall plant in corner) and* D. deremensis warneckei.

sun you will be limited to shade plants, or else you will have to add supplementary artificial light (see Chapter 12).

On the wall of my dining room that is opposite the window, I hung up an empty Coke-bottle case, thinking this would be a good place to root cuttings in small bottles and vials of water. It was a good idea, except there isn't enough light on this wall which is 12 feet back from the partly sunny window. Avocado pits sprout here perfectly, but most cuttings grow so spindly they die before they can form a root system. So far as I am concerned, and I have done it, if you have to scrimp in order to afford a sunny apartment, it's worth it if you want to grow plants.

Specific light and sun preferences are given with each

Author

My living room receives direct sunlight several feet inside during winter when the sun is low in its orbit. However, the weeping fig (Ficus benjamina) *in the foreground and pineapple plant with variegated foliage on the coffee table grow essentially on bright daylight alone.*

26

of the plants discussed in Chapter 10. Kinds that grow well
with bright light, but little or no sun shining directly on
them, include:

Aglaonema (Chinese evergreen)
Aspidistra (cast-iron plant)
Calathea
Chlorophytum (spider plant)
Cissus (grape-ivy and kangaroo vine)
Cryptanthus (earth-star bromeliad)
Cyperus (umbrella plant)
Davallia (rabbit's-foot fern)
Dracaena
Hedera (English ivy)
Helxine (baby's-tears)
Hoya (wax plant)
Maranta (prayer plant)
Nephrolepis (Boston fern)
Ophiopogon (lily-turf)
Persea (avocado)
Philodendron (some, but not all kinds)
Platycerium (staghorn fern)
Polypodium (bear's-paw fern)
Saintpaulia (African violet)
Sansevieria (snake plant)
Scindapsus (pothos)
Spathiphyllum (peace lily)
Syngonium (nephthytis or "Trileaf Wonder")
Tolmiea (piggyback plant)
Trevesia (snowflake plant)

I am not going to give listings of plants for sunny exposures, since even the shade-lovers can be grown close to,
if not directly in, such a window. Of course, the time of
year has to be considered also. Direct sun in the summer
is hotter than in the same window in winter. For this rea-

son, you may find that African violets grow to perfection and bloom profusely in a sunny south or west window in fall and winter, but as the days grow longer in the spring and through summer, they may need to be moved back as much as several feet to where there is less direct sun.

This observation brings up a question: How can you tell if a plant needs more or less light or direct sun? Light-starved plants look like you feel in the middle of winter when your friends return from ten days of sun in the West Indies. More specifically, plants in need of more light or sun tend to be paler—and sometimes darker—green than before. A sun-grown wax begonia stands up nicely with leaves about an inch apart along the stem. If it needs more light or sun, the same wax begonia will have leaves spaced up to two inches apart on the stem, and soon this stem will arch over, probably in the direction facing the source of strongest light. In really low light, the same plant might stop growing entirely, or begin to grow weak new leaves about the color of a beansprout taken from a dark closet. In other words, we're down to basic botany, about which I know little, except that plants need light in order to manufacture chlorophyll or green coloration.

Now that I've admitted to knowing little of botany, I think it's only fair for me to say that I have been success-ful in growing plants ever since I can remember. What I know of botany I have soaked up by osmosis, either from growing thousands of different plants, or possibly from editing even more thousands of pages of various garden writers' manuscripts. The truth is, the specific needs of most plants cultivated in pots indoors are recorded in countless books like this one. If you follow one of these as carefully as you would a new recipe, the chances are your plant will grow. It's that simple. So far as I am concerned, botany may help you grow better plants, it may even fascinate you, but it is not a prerequisite to being a good gardener.

What happens when a plant receives too much sun? It shows signs of sunburn just as surely as you do when over-exposed. African violets turn pale, yellowish green, and sometimes spots are actually burned in a leaf so that in a few days they turn dry, papery, and light brown. The dark green leaves of spathiphyllum and *Ficus elastica* (rubber tree) first develop a spot or edge along the leaf that is yellow, and after a few days this will begin to turn papery and medium to dark brown or black. The discolored part is dead; there is nothing you can do except to trim off the dead part with a pair of scissors and move the plant so that it receives less direct sun.

In the previous paragraph I mentioned *Ficus elastica,* not that I am a Latin namedropper, but so that you would know I was talking about the rubber tree and not about *Crassula argentea,* which is sometimes called rubber plant. In Chapter 10 I have listed the plants according to their true, botanical names, but all are cross-referenced by their common names. The trend today is so strongly toward calling plants by their botanical names that when I make a personal appearance, I realize I am more likely to give more information to the person who asks about a plant by its Latin name than if a popular name is given. I don't mean to be snobbish about it, I just know that if a person has gone to the trouble to learn a plant's true name, he or she will have probably also looked up its needs in a book and tried to meet them. This makes me want to try even harder to help solve whatever problem with the plant the person has asked me about. The Anglicized Latin phonetic pronunciations I give for each plant are in the easy style I learned from the late Ralph Bailey when I edited his 16-volume *Good Housekeeping Illustrated Encyclopedia of*

Gardening. If spathiphyllum scares you, try spath-uh-FILL-um. Or how about aechmea? Try ECK-mee-uh. It really is easy, and using the Latin names for plants will definitely cast a better light on you as an indoor gardener in any company.

Besides, as my friend Mary Jo says, "Did your mother ever call you by your nickname when she was having a serious talk with you? I'm afraid to talk to my plants for fear I'll tell them something they have no business knowing, but if I did, I would say, '*Dracaena fragrans,* if you don't stop dropping leaves, you'll never grow up to be a decent corn plant,' or whatever." Like Mary Jo, I'm not much of a talker to my plants, and probably for the same reason: We like the quiet time we spend with our plants, precisely because they respond to us, but without demanding spoken words in reply. Of course, neither of us always feels good things from our plants. Sometimes they show by a definite sign language that they are in trouble; for how to interpret what your plants may be saying to you, please see Chapter 9.

In specifying the light requirements of individual plants in Chapter 10 I have tried to indicate as broad a range as possible without being too general. If the light or sun needs are critical, then I indicate this with the plant's "*Environmental Needs.*" Most plants cultivated indoors tolerate a wide range of light or sun, especially if the rest of the environment is friendly.

In most of my earlier writings, I have indicated the light needs of plants as *sunny, semisunny, semishady,* and *shady.* In the terms of this book, these may be loosely interpreted as follows:

> *Sunny:* An unobstructed south-facing window.
> *Semisunny:* An unobstructed west-facing window.

Semishady: An unobstructed east-facing window.

Shady: A bright north-facing window.

In practice, the *sunny* exposure can be all of these, since sun-loving plants can serve as sun screens for the shade plants, and the shade-lovers can also be placed to the side, below, or back from the areas of the window that receive full sun. To a lesser extent this is also true of the *semi-sunny* and *semishady* windows.

If you have more sun plants than you have sunny space, try rotating them so that each receives a fair share. Growth will not be the same as if each received maximum sun, but all should enjoy satisfactory health.

LIGHT TIPS. If you're giving a plant everything it needs in terms of proper soil moisture, humidity, temperature, and fertilizer, and still it does not grow to suit you, try giving it more or less light or sun.

Large, mature plants of many kinds are good keepers in less light or sun than they have grown accustomed to, for example, beaucarnea (ponytail plant), philodendron, monstera, most palms cultivated in pots, dieffenbachia (dumbcane), most bromeliads and spathiphyllum. However, if the light or sun is too deficient, new growth will be pale, unnaturally small, even malformed or nonexistent. *Ficus benjamina* (weeping fig) and coleus on the other hand are not good keepers in poor light; within hours or days they will begin to drop older leaves, which is their sign language way of saying they need more light or sun.

Once they are in full bloom, many seasonal flowering plants, such as amaryllis, bromeliad, chrysanthemum, tulip, hyacinth, and cineraria, will last longer if no sun shines directly on them. However, in order to be brought into bloom they do require direct sun. Slightly more complicated is the gloxinia purchased in bloom from a florist. The flowers that have opened already will probably last longer if no sun shines directly on them; however, if there are buds still growing from the center of the plant, they need some sun, especially in winter, in order to mature into beautiful blossoms.

All window plants will grow more shapely if the containers in which they grow are given a quarter or half turn once a week so that all sides of the plant enjoy the benefits of maximum light or sun. Since more than 300 plants grow in my apartment, I would be the first to admit that I do not turn every pot and hanging basket once a week. In practice, they get turned when I happen to think about it, or when company is coming and I want the best sides of all to face into the room.

Once you become aware of the light and sun patterns in the rooms where you live and work, you will be much better able to situate plants so that they will thrive from the beginning, instead of growing light-starved or sun-burned and losing their good looks if not good health before you find the right light for them.

3. Temperatures for Plant Comfort

Most house plants grow well in temperatures that are comfortable for you. In the centrally heated and cooled spaces in which the majority of us live and work, this means a temperature range of 62–75 degrees. The specific needs for each plant are given in Chapter 10 under its *Environmental Needs*.

The only way you can be sure of the temperature range where your plants are growing is to use a thermometer, preferably of the maximum-minimum type so that you will know the extremes of hot and cold in any given 24-hour period. By using a thermometer you will be able to locate the little climates of hot and cold, and thereby know where to situate plants that need coolness or extra warmth. I once lived in a high-rise apartment building with all-glass exterior walls. At the bottom of each six- by six-foot fixed pane was a smaller window that could be opened. One of these had a faulty latch which permitted a breeze of fresh air to enter. Because I kept forgetting to ask the maintenance man to repair it, I discovered that this provided a little climate with cooler temperatures in winter where I could grow several pots of cyclamen and primroses that stayed in bloom for months instead of weeks as they would have in the adjoining, warmer windows.

Contrary to what you may have heard, central air conditioning causes house plants surprisingly little discomfort. In my apartment, plants grow all around the heating-cooling units, the same as they do at *House Beautiful* where most of the editors have windows filled with thriving, flowering plants, African violets included. What seems more vital is soil that is always nicely moist, never bone dry, and not soggy wet for more than a few hours at a time.

What house plants do not like are hot, dry drafts of air. The main trouble area in most apartments and offices is directly over a heating unit, especially near the ceiling where hanging baskets are sometimes hung. By the same token, tropical plants that like a warm atmosphere in winter suffer when placed next to a window that for one reason or another allows drafts of really cold air to blow on them. Of course, there are plants that like cool air; these are indicated in Chapter 10.

The one kind of heat I have not mentioned is the old-fashioned steam or hot-water radiator over which you may have little or no control. One simple solution in this situation is to cover the radiator surface with Pyrex cas-

34

seroles filled with pebbles and water. The bottom heat causes the water to evaporate, and the result is a more humid atmosphere which helps plants thrive. You can also have a two-inch-deep galvanized metal tray made to fit on top of the radiator. Fill the tray with pebbles. Add water often enough to keep it just slightly below the pebble surface so that pot bases will be above the water level and not in it; otherwise, they may soak up too much moisture which could cause the roots to rot for lack of air.

One thing for certain, almost all house plants need some fresh air that circulates freely. Stale air is no better for plants than it is for you. I had read this kind of advice for years before its importance registered on me. Eventually I realized that my plants grew much better both in the spring and in the fall during the periods of time when neither heat nor cold was being circulated through the building air-conditioning system. For reasons of human comfort during these times I would open the windows during the daytime, and often at night. Now, during the summer, I raise some of the windows at night so that my plants receive some fresh air, and during the winter I open a window in each room just slightly on warm days for the same reason. This is usually less a problem in a single-family residence where doors open directly to the outdoors and permit fresh air to enter each time someone comes or goes. In an apartment the door opens to a hallway where the air is even staler than that inside.

However desirable it may be, being able to open a door or window directly to the outdoors is not essential to healthy plant growth. There are many office buildings which have sealed windows that can never be opened. This is true at *House Beautiful,* yet the windows are filled with hundreds of thriving plants. This is the situation

35

found in most office buildings today which, viewed from outdoors at night with the lights on inside, appear increasingly to be giant greenhouses.

One way to keep air moving among your plants is to use a small circulating fan, preferably of the oscillating type. This is especially helpful in a small room where many plants are cultivated, and essential if you have situated a fluorescent-light garden in a closet. It can also be a help to you as well as your plants if you work in a small office where the building air-conditioning system is not as effective as you would like.

A side benefit of air that circulates constantly is that plant stems subjected to constant slight movement grow shorter and sturdier than those in still air. For this reason, commercial growers keep the air circulating among potted chrysanthemum plants so that they will mature as short and compact as possible, while the grower of long-stemmed roses for cutting keeps the air as still as possible to achieve the opposite effect.

4. A Pleasantly Moist Atmosphere Is Good for Your Plants—and You

At the height of the winter heating season, most houses, apartments, and offices have an atmosphere that is about as moist as a dried-up sponge. This lack of moisture, or humidity, in the air makes it difficult for you to breathe, the joints of fine wood furniture may draw apart and the leaves of all but the toughest plants wither and dry along the edges and tips.

The only way to tell for sure how much humidity there is is to use a hygrometer which will give you a read-out in numbers that represent the percentage of relative humidity in the atmosphere. Generally speaking, the hotter the air, the lower the percentage of relative humidity.

Clear plastic picture frames from the dimestore (cardboards first removed) are used here as pebble trays in a north-facing apartment window.

Hygrometers are sold by hardware stores; they are available by mail from the House Plant Corner (see Chapter 11).

In a space heated to around 75 degrees by forced hot air or a radiator, it is not unusual to find the humidity hovering around 5 percent. This is not enough for you, your furniture or your plants. Pianos in particular suffer in hot, dry air. The good news is that by raising the humidity you can lower the heat and be more comfortable than before. This cuts down on fuel costs, and at the same time tends to reduce respiratory discomforts. It also helps the piano stay in tune, reduces stress on antique wood furniture, and fosters better plant growth.

The simplest way to increase humidity for your plants

is to group them on shallow trays filled with pebbles and water. The only rule to remember about this arrangement is to keep the water at a level slightly below where the base of each pot rests, otherwise through the process of osmosis the soil will take up too much moisture and may become water-logged, a condition that can lead to rotted, drowned roots.

Trays may be plastic, glass, or galvanized metal. You can find them in plant shops, garden centers, nurseries, or wherever housewares are sold. Some humidity trays on the market, designed specifically to fit on a window sill, are only an inch deep, but ideally a humidity tray should be about two inches deep, and always waterproof. Caught in a bind with a quantity of new plants in two- and three-inch pots, I have used cookie sheets and even the cannisters in which video tapes and motion pictures are distributed, which I have found discarded on the streets of New York, but the problem with these is that they soon rust, and may leave ugly discoloration on the floor or other surface on which they have been resting.

You can fill a humidity tray with marble chips, washed river pebbles, sand, perlite, or vermiculite. I prefer the chips or pebbles since they do not adhere to the pot bottoms and are therefore less likely to cause a mess when plants are moved.

Another easy way to increase humidity is to keep large, open containers of water placed on top of the radiator or other heating unit, and among plants. Pyrex casseroles are especially useful for this purpose, and since they are ovenproof, there is no danger that they will become overheated. Decorative colored glass bottles of water may also be set among plants, but the smaller the opening or surface of water exposed to the air, the less moisture will evaporate.

Misting your plants with tepid water is an excellent way

to increase humidity, and since you cannot mist them without being in close proximity, a side benefit is that you will also be able to check at the same time to see if they need some water added to the soil, or if they need other attentions. There are all kinds of hand-operated misters on the market. The first ones to become popular were the small copper or polished chrome misters which hold about one cup of water. These are fine if you have only a few plants. However, if you are reading this book, you are probably ready for a more serious piece of equipment, either a plastic mister that holds a pint or quart of water, or one of the battery-powered units that holds up to a gallon of water. One side benefit of misting regularly with one of these is that once every two weeks or so you can fill it with water to which a foliar fertilizer such as Ra-Pid-Gro has been added. And once every two weeks you can also fill the mister with a mixture of water and Dr. Bronner's Peppermint Soap (available from health-food stores), mixed in the proportions recommended on the soap container. This serves as an excellent, organic deterrent to insects.

If you are depending on misting alone to raise the humidity around your plants, you'll have to mist faithfully once a day and preferably twice. As much as I might like to do this, or enjoy doing it, I don't have time. My plants are lucky if they get misted two or three times a week. For this reason, I use cool-vapor humidifiers in my apartment throughout the winter heating season.

The simplest, least expensive cool-vapor humidifier is the type sold by drugstores and pharmacies for use in the treatment of respiratory illnesses. Do not confuse a cool-vapor humidifier with the type that dispenses a mist of hot water or steam. The only drawback to a room-size cool-vapor humidifier, which costs around $20, is that it likely will hold two gallons of water at most, and this may be

At Greenleaves plant shop in New York City, Karen Jacobus uses a hand-pump type pressure sprayer to mist a giant staghorn fern.

41

misted into the atmosphere within 12 hours, which means that twice a day you will have to refill it in order to keep up the beneficial misting. If you don't mind having to do this, a cool-vapor humidifier of this size can be highly

Black & Decker

A battery-powered sprayer (plug it in overnight and the battery re-charges) is an excellent way to efficiently and easily mist a quantity of house plants.

effective in increasing the moisture content of an average-size room.

The next step up in humidifiers is to buy an apartment-size unit which holds six to eight gallons of water and will need to be filled once every two or three days. I use one of these in my living room which also humidifies the air in the dining area, and during the coldest weather when the forced-air heat is required constantly I use a room-size humidifier in each of the two bedrooms. With all of these going, average humidity ranges between 40 and 60 percent, and keeps all of my plants in good health, including orchids, gesneriads, and bromeliads.

Although a range of 40–60 percent humidity may sound like I live in a damp, musty-smelling apartment, the result is exactly the opposite. With this amount of humidity I can keep the forced-air heating units turned on low instead of high, and the air smells fresh and pleasantly moist. The piano definitely sounds better than it does with less humidity, we breathe more easily, and the plants grow much better.

Although it is not difficult to obtain room-size humidifiers locally, they are listed in the mail-order catalog of the House Plant Corner (see Chapter 11). Apartment-size humidifiers are sold by appliance stores, or they can be ordered from major catalog retailers (Sears, for example).

One thing I have not mentioned is that the more plants you have, the more moisture they give off into the atmosphere. I use 10–20 gallons of water weekly to keep my collection of approximately 300 plants moist. Obviously, a lot of moisture is being evaporated into the atmosphere of my apartment.

5. How Much and How Often to Water

Having placed a sheet of blank paper in my typewriter to begin this chapter, I began to formulate what I wanted to say. Inevitably, when the right words do not come in a flash, I decide my plants need to be watered, groomed, or repotted. Today, as I write in my office at *House Beautiful,* it just so happens that the plants have all been recently repotted and groomed, so the only way I could procrastinate was to water them. Fortunately, they needed to be watered, and what I want to say in this chapter is now clearly fixed in my mind. The only problem is that I seem to have splashed a generous amount of water on my manuscript paper.

How did I know the plants needed to be watered? Well, for one thing, the fancy-leaved Cyclone impatiens plant was wilted. I saw it the instant I walked into my office. The leaves were hanging down in total dejection. I dropped the shopping bag I was carrying and, still wearing my raindrop-dripping slicker, I raced off to fill the watering can. Now, less than an hour later, the impatiens is standing happily erect, just as if it had enjoyed walking with me in the rain outdoors. Unfortunately, it dried out enough that most of the older leaves and the flower buds have withered beyond recovery.

There are two lessons here about watering plants: (1) *No matter how much it rains outdoors, house plants depend entirely on us for water,* and (2) *if you wait to water a plant until it is visibly wilted, older leaves will wither and die prematurely along with tender new growth, especially flower buds.* This second statement applies in particular to zebra-plant (aphelandra), coleus, and any flowering florist plant in full bloom such as chrysanthemum, gardenia, gloxinia, azalea, cineraria, poinsettia, hydrangea, daffodil, paperwhite narcissus, tulip, and hyacinth. To complicate things, not all plants wilt visibly when they are dry. Dwarf citrus (calamondin, for example), jasmine, and ficus just quietly drop quantities of leaves, often while they are still a healthy green color.

The great misconception about watering house plants comes from the advice to let a plant "dry out" before you water it again. What the purveyors of this recommendation mean to say is that the soil should *dry out slightly* or *approach dryness* before more water is added. The truth is that even desert plants such as cacti and other succulents should never dry out completely.

When the soil in any pot dries out completely, the roots suffer irreparable damage. When you saturate this dry soil with water, most if not all of the roots will have

46

Moisture meters of this type have a long probe which you stick into the soil. The read-out on the dial tells you whether or not to add water.

already withered to the point of no return; they can no longer absorb moisture. The result is that they rot. If all of the roots suffer this fate, the entire plant dies. If only part of the roots die, probably only a part of the plant will die. This can be seen quite clearly in a tree-size weeping fig (*Ficus benjamina*) that grows in a pot or tub 12 inches in diameter or larger. If only part of the soil is moistened at the time of watering, pockets of completely dry soil will exist within the same container. The result is that entire branches of the tree may die, while others remain perfectly healthy. The pocket of dry soil is directly related to the dried-up branches. This illus-

47

trates lesson 3 about watering plants: *Apply enough water so that all of the soil and roots are well moistened.* How much water you have to apply in order to do this varies according to the size and kind of pot, the size of the plant, the type of soil and the moisture content of the soil at the time of watering.

SIZE AND KIND OF POT. Two- and three-inch pots (measure across the top) need approximately one-fourth cup water to moisten the soil and roots; four- and five-inch pots need approximately one-half cup of water; six- and seven-inch pots need approximately one cup of water; 8- to 10-inch pots need approximately two cups of water. Larger sizes may need one to two quarts of water. Plants growing in unglazed, ordinary clay flowerpots tend to need more water than those growing in plastic, glazed ceramic, or other pots, the walls of which are sealed and therefore do not soak up or evaporate moisture.

SIZE OF THE PLANT. This relates directly to the size of the pot in which the plant is growing. In other words, a small plant in a large pot of soil will require less frequent watering than a large plant that is growing in a small pot. This is especially important when you are dealing with a newly purchased plant which may have filled the pot of soil in which it is growing with roots. Until you feel confident about this yourself, ask the person who sells you the plant if it needs to be moved to a size larger pot. If in doubt, remove the pot and have a look. Take the pot and plant in one hand, and with your palm and fingers placed around the base of the plant and across the soil surface, turn it upside down. If the pot does not come off easily when you give it a firm tug with your other hand, tap the edge of the pot on a table or other solid surface. If the plant needs a size larger pot and some fresh soil, you will see that its roots have filled the present soil; they will be visible all around the outside of the soil and some may have grown through the drainage hole of the pot.

TYPE OF SOIL. Once they have been saturated, sticky, heavy, clayey soils require less water less often than soils that contain quantities of perlite or sand which make soil better aerated. Potting soils that contain quantities of vermiculite and peat moss tend to be well aerated, and at the same time they retain moisture. Since most of us grow house plants in a variety of different soil mixtures, the only way to tell for sure when water is needed is to poke your finger into the surface soil and see if it feels wet, moist, or dry.

MOISTURE CONTENT OF SOIL AT WATERING TIME. If the soil surface feels wet when you touch it, no additional water is needed. If the soil surface feels moist, again no additional water is needed—unless you are about to leave the plant unattended for a couple of days or more, in which case you should water the plant well, but after an hour pour off any water remaining in the saucer. If the soil surface feels bone dry, apply water immediately.

The main rule to remember about watering has to do with a pot or other container in which the surface soil feels bone dry when you feel it. This may mean that the soil and roots have dried to the point of shrinking away from the walls of the pot. When you apply water it will tend to run across the surface, down between the shrunken soil and rootball, right out the drainage hole without actually penetrating the main mass of roots and soil. The way to water such a plant is to set the pot in a deep saucer, bowl, basin, or pail of water and leave it to soak until beads of moisture show on the surface. Then remove, allow to drain for a few minutes, and return to where it had been growing before. If the plant is too large to move, keep adding water to its saucer until it soaks up no more. At this point, do not continue to leave it standing in a saucer of water; use a bulb baster from the kitchen to draw off the excess.

The water you use to moisten house plants should always be of room temperature, or slightly warmer, as in "tepid." This is especially important in the winter when water taken directly from the faucet is likely to be ice cold, and definitely not to the liking of any house plant whose ancestors came from the tropics. What about the chemicals contained by faucet water? If the water is fit for human consumption, it's fine for house plants. Purists use rain or snow water warmed to room temperature, or leave water from the faucet standing overnight in a pail or watering can so that gasses from chemical additives can evaporate, but frankly, I don't have time to follow either of these practices.

How often and how much to water a potted plant is perhaps an even bigger puzzle to the beginner than the amount of light or sun needed. In the question-answer sessions that follow most of my lectures, I am inevitably asked, "Why can't garden writers say exactly how much and how often to water each plant?" The answer is that there are too many variables for any given plant, some of which include the time of year, age and size of the plant, the kind of soil in which it is growing, temperatures in the room, quantity of light or sun, and whether the pot walls are porous or sealed. Poking your finger into the surface soil is one sure way to tell if a plant needs water, as I have discussed earlier in this chapter.

The more scientific approach for judging soil moisture needs is to use a soil moisture meter such as the Sav-a-Plant (widely distributed by mail-order companies and available at many retail plant shops). Meters of this type have a long probe which you insert deep into the pot to determine moisture content where most of the roots live instead of on the surface where dryness may not necessarily indicate that soil deeper in the pot is also dry. What you should probably avoid using are cheap paper-and-plastic labels which theoretically tell you when a plant is wet or dry, but which in practice are virtually useless.

What about automated plant watering systems? Some

Bill Mulligan

Although bromeliads like this neoregelia need slightly moist soil, it is important to keep fresh water filling the cup formed by the leaves. Once a week, pour out the old water in preparation for adding new.

work and some don't. My preference is to do the watering myself, partly because I enjoy taking care of my plants, and partly because I like to cater to the moisture needs of each. However, if watering is your nemesis with plants, or if you travel a great deal and are away from home for periods of a week or more and have no one to act as your plantsitter, it may be worth your while to try automatic watering devices. Most on the market operate on the double-wall principle, meaning the pot itself is designed to hold a quantity of water which it releases automatically into the soil depending on the needs of the plant. I don't fault the theory behind the design, only the fact that some products on the market work better than others. The only way to proceed is to look at what is available, invest in one container of the type you like best and try it. If the results are satisfactory, then you can feel confident in buying the same type container for all of your plants.

What about watering plants when you're away from home and do not have some kind of automated system? I'm asked this question a lot because people know I travel constantly and that I have several hundred plants. Since I share my apartment with two other adults, almost always at least one of us is at home to do the watering. If we're all away at the same time, I can now rely on my teenaged children who live nearby with their mother and have become fine plantsitters. And occasionally when we all go away together, I ask my secretary to come in and do the honors.

If I lived alone, or did not have family and friends to take care of my plants, here are some suggestions for how I would solve the problem:

(1) Engage the services of a professional plantsitter the same as you would a dog walker. If the person is

Bill Mulligan

After emptying old water out of a bromeliad, re-fill the cup formed by the leaves with fresh. This plant is Aechmea chantinii.

truly qualified, you may come home to healthier plants than before.

(2) Arrange to have some employee of your apartment building come in regularly to water the plants. If they are obviously inexperienced and worried about the assignment, stick a label in each pot with watering instructions indicating specific frequency and quantity for every plant. For example: "1 cup water Mondays and Thursdays." As you will quickly realize, this is arbitrary, but at least it is better than a strictly hit-or-miss procedure.

(3) If you must leave your plants unattended, group small pots together in a waterproof tray. Saturate the soil just before you leave, adding enough water so that the pot bases stand in about a half inch of water. This should sustain the plants for 7 to 10 days. You may lose one or two from overwatering, but surprisingly enough, most will survive. Saturate the soil in larger pots and when it will accept no more water, fill the saucer. Again, the plant should be able to survive for up to two weeks or more. If the winter heating system is on, turn it back as much as possible, probably to 50 or 55 degrees. This saves on the amount of moisture that will evaporate in your absence.

(4) Another system you can try when you must leave your plants unattended for periods of a week or more is to enclose them in large, clear plastic bags. If the plants normally grow in an exposure where they receive several hours of direct sun, move them away from the window so that they receive bright light but little or no direct sun, otherwise they may become too steamy hot inside the plastic. Before you enclose a plant in plastic, be sure to remove any dead or yellowed leaves, open or spent flowers. This helps prevent disease problems which could occur in the constantly humid environment. Also check to

be sure there are no insects on plants before you enclose them in plastic.

WATERING TIPS. When you discover a plant is severely dry, either by its wilted appearance, or by touching the soil, move it out of direct sunlight immediately and water well. Do not apply fertilizer to dry soil.

If you find a plant has been standing in water for so long that the soil smells stagnant, remove the pot immediately. Working carefully, extricate the roots from the spoiled soil, then rinse them in water of room temperature. Cut away and discard any that appear to be discolored and rotted. Repot in fresh soil that is nicely moist; return to where the plant has been growing. If it shows any signs of wilting, enclose in clear plastic and keep out of direct sun until the leaves perk up. Throw away the old soil.

6. Soil, Soil Substitutes, and Food for Your Plants

Mixing up potting soil for your plants is like making pastry: You start with a recipe and in no time at all you will learn to vary proportions to get just the right feel or consistency to produce the desired results. Actually, special mixing isn't necessary if you want to rely on commercially packaged potting soils. However, unless you have access to a mixture prepared by an expert for exactly the kind of plant you are growing, it may be better to combine a packaged potting soil with one or more additional ingredients such as vermiculite or perlite. This is not difficult to learn. In fact, you will find it a satisfying experience to actually dig your hands into the various

57

growing mediums, feel their textures, and see how your plants respond to different combinations.

Wherever plants are sold, you will find packages of potting soil. Usually these are labeled in such a way as to suggest the kinds of plants for which each is best suited. There are many different trade names, and contents and consistencies vary considerably, but the general guidelines that follow will give you the basic understanding you need to succeed with any of them.

ALL-PURPOSE POTTING SOIL. Essentially, just what the name implies. Most house plants will live in this kind of soil without mixing in additives. However, these tend to be too dense, heavy, and poorly drained to produce plants that truly thrive. There are exceptions, of course. Notably, I have found that Chinese evergreens (species

Author

Soil mixture ingredients you are likely to encounter and find useful; upper row, left to right, perlite, charcoal chips, milled (screened) sphagnum moss; lower row, left to right, vermiculite, sand and all-purpose potting soil mixed with other ingredients according to directions in the text.

and varieties of *Aglaonema*) and snake plants (species and varieties of *Sansevieria*) grow well in all-purpose potting soils used exactly as they come from the bag.

For most flowering and foliage plants, cacti and other succulents excepted, I follow this recipe for improving all-purpose potting soil:

> 2 parts all-purpose potting soil
> 1 part sphagnum peat moss
> 1 part vermiculite
> 1 part perlite

In practice, you might thus mix together two cups all-purpose potting soil with one cup *each* sphagnum peat moss, vermiculite, and perlite.

For cacti and other succulents, and plants that tend to be epiphytic (bromeliads in particular which in nature often perch themselves up in the air in crotches formed by tree branches where they depend on frequent tropical rains for sustenance), I follow this recipe for amending all-purpose potting soil:

> 1 part all-purpose potting soil
> 1 part sphagnum peat moss
> 1 part vermiculite
> 2 parts perlite

CACTUS POTTING SOIL. As it comes from the bag, a mixture so labeled will probably be fairly sandy, in combination with some soil and peat moss. It should be well-drained, meaning that water drains through it quickly and the roots receive more air than if they were growing in straight all-purpose potting soil to which no other ingredients had been added. Occasionally a commercially packaged cactus potting soil will become hard and crusty, almost like cement, after it has been watered. If this should happen, unpot the plant and carefully wash off any of the soil adhering to the roots. Try adding one part vermiculite to three parts of the cactus soil; mix together well, then repot the plant. This should correct the problem. Otherwise, cactus potting soil should be satisfactory for cacti and other succulents when used just as it comes from the bag.

AFRICAN VIOLET POTTING SOIL. These are usually high in humus content (sphagnum peat moss, for example), and slightly acid on the soil pH scale, which is to the liking of African violets, related plants such as gloxinias, columneas and other gesneriads, plus begonias, dwarf citrus, azaleas, and gardenias. I find that most common foliage plants do well in packaged African violet soil, including ferns, philodendrons, dracaenas, and spathiphyllums. Although various brand names are available whereever plants are sold, probably the best in the world is put up by the Buell Greenhouses and can be ordered by mail (see Chapter 11 for address).

TERRARIUM SOIL. I have tried a number of these, all with satisfactory results for terrarium, bottle, and bowl gardens. Quite frankly, I can't tell the difference between packaged terrarium soil and packaged African violet soil. I have used terrarium soils for potting up African violets, gloxinias, begonias, coleus, and any number of other house plants, all with good results.

Now we come to the additives you'll find in packages wherever growing supplies for house plants are sold. I try to keep a supply of all these on hand, for reasons I will explain in the text which follows.

VERMICULITE. This is expanded natural mica which is mined from the earth. Long before we used it for growing plants, builders used vermiculite for insulation and as a concrete aggregate. It is sterile and my favorite medium for starting cuttings and seeds of all plants, both indoors and outdoors. In a well-stocked garden center you may find vermiculite in fine, medium, and coarse grades. The particles of fine vermiculite are slightly larger than those of coarse builders' sand. I prefer the medium grade for starting seeds and cuttings, and as an additive to potting soils, although the coarse is also excellent for mixing into a sticky, heavy soil to make it spongier and better aerated. Potting soil recipes in older books often call for well-rotted leaf mold, something difficult to obtain unless you have access to a wooded area, but medium or coarse vermiculite makes an excellent substitute.

PERLITE. Like vermiculite, perlite is also a natural material mined from the earth and, in its processed form, a widely used additive to potting soil mixture. It is white, granular, and almost weightless. I use it as a substitute for sand in various combinations with all-purpose potting soil, peat moss, and vermiculite. Perlite, as it comes from the bag, is sterile. It can be used alone for rooting cuttings, but I prefer vermiculite.

PEAT MOSS. Essentially there are two kinds of peat moss packaged and sold for plants. One is coarse, brown, and fibrous and called sphagnum peat moss. This is the kind to use in making potting mixes for house plants. The other is dark brown, almost black when moistened, and very fine or powdery, with only a few twigs mixed in. This type of peat moss is undesirable for adding to potting soils. When added to all-purpose potting soil, sphagnum peat moss makes it more spongy, more water retentive, and better aerated, all at the same time. I have had excellent results in growing seeds and rooting cuttings in a mixture of equal parts peat moss and vermiculite. If you mix together equal parts of peat moss, vermiculite, and perlite, the result will be close to some of the newly popular soil-less growing mediums, discussed later in this chapter.

CHARCOAL CHIPS. These are now considered *de rigueur* as an additive to any potting soil that will be placed in a container that has no bottom drainage, such as

61

a terrarium, bottle or bowl garden. Within reason, charcoal chips have the ability to keep constantly moist, undrained soil fresh and pleasant to smell—and therefore conducive to healthy root growth. I add a handful of charcoal chips to each quart of potting soil destined for a container that has no provision for drainage of excess moisture.

SAND. Most sand available in packages today is intended more for decorative effect, as in sand painting or to carpet the surface of a desertscape of cacti and other succulents, and not as an additive to potting soil. The kind of sand to use in growing mediums is clean, sharp, or builders'. Do not use sand from the seashore as it contains too much salt. Perlite, as I have mentioned earlier, is an excellent substitute for sand.

MARBLE CHIPS AND PEBBLES. These are packaged to be used as an inch-deep, bottom layer for drainage in pots, tubs, and planters approximately 10 inches and larger in diameter. They are also ideal for filling humidity trays (see Chapter 4) and to use as a final surface layer or dressing around potted cacti and other succulents. Before using either marble chips or pebbles, it is a good idea to put them in a large kitchen sieve or collander and run water through for a minute or two to wash away dust and particles of soil.

OSMUNDA FIBER AND BARK CHIPS. These mediums are used primarily for growing orchids and bromeliads. They are seldom available locally, but you can order them from mail-order specialists in these plants (see Chapter 11 for addresses).

TOTEM POLES. These are available as slabs of tree-fern bark (similar in appearance to the osmunda fiber in which orchids are cultivated) and as pieces of bark-covered wood. Climbing philodendrons and pothos in particular do best if they have a totem pole on which to

Measure fertilizer exactly according to directions on the label. It is better not to apply a fertilizer solution to severely dry soil; moisten it first with water, then a few days later apply fertilizer if the plant appears to have suffered no great shock from dry soil.

climb; for best results, mist the pole daily so that it will be moist enough to be inviting for the air roots of the plant to attach themselves to the surface.

In recent years soil-less, peat-like, synthetic growing mediums have come into wide use by commercial as well as amateur growers. Most of the ones available wherever plants are sold are based on formulas developed at either Cornell University or the University of California. As they come from the bag, all of these are sterile and as nearly as I can tell they contain little or no nutrients to foster growth. However, when used in combination with constant feeding, results can be phenomenal. Some of the popular trade names include Jiffy-Mix, Redi-Earth, Pro-Mix, Supersoil, and University Formula. When I use one of these, I feed the plant with every watering, diluting the plant food to about one-fourth the usual strength. For example, if the container directions call for 1 teaspoon fertilizer to 1 quart of water, reduce this to ¼ teaspoon fertilizer to 1 quart of water for feeding with every watering. I have also obtained excellent results with soil-less mixes by applying precise timed-release fertilizer pellets to the surface according to the directions on the container.

Earlier in this chapter I recommended the potting soil of Buell's Greenhouses for growing African violets, gloxinias, and other gesneriads. An equally fine, but soil-less mixture for growing gesneriads (including African violets and gloxinias) and begonias, called G-B-S Growing Mix, is available by mail from grower Michael Kartuz (see Chapter 11 for address). If you'd like to mix your own, here is his recipe:

2 parts sphagnum moss, screened
1 quart Terra-Lite vermiculite
1 quart coarse perlite (Sponge Rok)
1 tablespoon ground limestone

Rub the peat moss through a ½-inch mesh hardware cloth sieve to remove lumps and small twigs. Canadian or European sphagnum moss should be used. Put all the ingredients in a suitable clean container and mix well. Moisten prior to use. The mix is ready to use immediately, or it can be stored indefinitely in a closed plastic bag or covered plastic garbage pail.

FEEDING YOUR PLANTS. Potted plants grow better more consistently if they are fed regularly. Those recently potted into fresh soil don't actually need to be fed for two or three months, but as soon as they are growing actively with no signs of transplanting shock (wilting, for example), it won't hurt to begin feeding them if you follow directions on the container of plant food.

Incidentally, the problem of sematics sometimes gets in

3M Company

Timed-release pellets are an easy, convenient way to give your potted plants a little fertilizer everytime you water them. One application lasts for four months.

the way when it come to feeding plants. Feeding is not the same as watering. House plants can't live without regular watering, but they will survive, although probably not thrive, without regular feeding.

The house plant fertilizer business is rapidly expanding, and countless formulations are on the market, some designed specifically for feeding with every watering, some formulated for feeding once every two weeks or once a month. Just be sure to read the label before you mix up the solution for feeding your plants. Generally speaking there are two types of house plant food on the market: all purpose and blooming (or flowering; often labeled specifically for African violets). All purpose will nurture healthy growth on all kinds of plants, foliage in particular. Blooming should promote flowering-type plants such as begonias and African violets to set buds and produce flowers.

FEEDING HINTS. Apply fertilizer only to soil that is nicely moist. Never feed a potted plant that is wilted as a result of dry soil. It is also best not to apply fertilizer to any plant that has recently suffered unusual stress, such as being moved from the ideal environment of a commercial greenhouse to your home, or if it has just been transplanted. Wait until the plant has adapted to its new environment before you begin feeding.

Plants known to require an acid soil, such as camellias, gardenias, and dwarf citrus, sometimes quite abruptly begin to turn a sickly yellowish-green color. This is their sign-language way of telling you that their soil has become too sweet or alkaline. Satisfy their needs by feeding with an acid-type fertilizer such as Stern's Mir-Acid (available at local garden centers, or by mail from Stern's; see Chapter 11 for address).

Most house plant foods are chemical creations. If organic gardening appeals to you, use a fish-emulsion type fertilizer. Middle-of-the-road indoor gardeners often alternate fertilizers, using a chemical type for one feeding, an organic for the next, and so forth. I have good results with all three practices.

Newly purchased house plants, especially large bushes and trees in sizable containers, have sometimes been fed with timed-release fertilizer pellets such as Osmocote before you buy them. Some growers are careful to label such plants so that you will know approximately when the pellets no longer contain nutrients and when you should begin adding fertilizer. However, not all plants treated with time-release fertilizer pellets are so labeled. If in doubt, scratch around in the surface soil. If pellets are present, you will see them as round, amber-colored particles, varying in size from about $\frac{1}{16}$ to $\frac{1}{8}$ inch in diameter. If you find these, don't panic; they are not insect eggs, but their presence does indicate that the plant should not be fed by you for at least three to four months.

If you are growing any plant in less than ideal light, or in temperatures not as warm as it would like, feed it much less than you would the same plant under normal circumstances, probably only once every two or three months.

7. Pots and Potting

We've come a long way from the days when it was thought that potted plants looked their best all tied up in ribbon and foil. Plant containers have come out of the closet to be what they are; in a few short years the utilitarian clay flowerpot has gone from not being accepted as a thing of beauty to becoming an example of timeless good taste, in the consideration of many designers. Of another age, but to my mind a near equal, is the white plastic pot designed along the same lines as classic clay. But if it's plastic, my esthetics say no scalloped edges, embossing to make it fit in with so-called Mediterranean decor, or stick-on decals.

Are unglazed clay or plastic pots better for plants? In

my experience, it makes no difference. Moisture evaporates through the walls of unglazed clay pots, and plants growing in them thus require more water than if they were growing in plastic. Also, because clay is porous, the pot edges tend to remain moist, and may in time collect mineral salts from water, soil and fertilizer—which may be harmful to plants like African violets whose leaf stems sometimes rest on the pot edges. Otherwise, clay or plastic, it makes no difference. Glazed ceramic pots with drainage holes in the bottom are equally useful for plants, and, as in plastic, soil dries out less quickly than in unglazed clay.

Probably the most important thing to remember about flowerpots is that culture is easiest if they have drainage holes in the bottom so that excess moisture can run off readily into the saucer or humidity tray underneath. When you want to grow a plant in a container which has no drainage hole, first add a layer of pebbles, gravel, or the peanutlike plastic foam pellets used for packing. This layer in the bottom should be equal to or slightly less than one-third the height of the container. Sprinkle a handful of charcoal chips on top of the drainage layer; they help keep the soil fresh even though excess moisture may be trapped occasionally in the drainage layer. I have to say that, in my experience, plants tend not to do as well in a container without a drainage hole or holes as they do in one with them. My preference is to grow the plant in a slightly smaller clay or plastic pot (of any color) which can be slipped inside the decorative container which has no drainage hole. If the rim of the growing pot is distracting, carpet the entire exposed soil surface and rim with pieces of florists' sheet moss. This gives a beautiful, natural finishing touch, but in order to tell when the plant needs water, you'll have to raise up a piece of the moss and feel the soil with your finger, or insert a moisture meter probe (discussed in Chapter 5).

This species Cat-tleya, one of the eas-ier orchids to grow, obviously needs re-potting—it is grow-ing right out of the present container.

Bill Mulligan

With the pot re-moved, you can see how the cattleya roots are practically strangling each other in search of new growing medium.

Bill Mulligan

Pull matted roots apart with your fin-gers, working gently so as to break as few as possible.

Bill Mulligan

Use a sharp knife to remove any broken or otherwise damaged roots, as well as any which appear to be shriveled, discolored or dead.
Bill Mulligan

If a plant has several stems arising from the soil, it can usually be divided; that is what is being done with this cattleya.
Bill Mulligan

For any plant which needs well-drained soil, it is standard practice to add a few pieces of broken clay pot or a layer of pebbles in the bottom of the new pot.
Bill Mulligan

Next add a generous layer of fresh potting soil.
Bill Mulligan

Position the roots so that the plant will grow at approximately the same level in relation to the soil surface and pot rim as it did before.
Bill Mulligan

Add handfuls of potting soil, gently but firmly pressing it in place about the roots.
Bill Mulligan

73

I've noticed that relatively small flowerpots are almost always used with a matching saucer, but larger containers (especially the metal and plastic cannisters often used by commercial growers) don't necessarily come with a saucer of suitable size—and large saucers can be expensive. However, I find they are a necessity. Without them it is only human nature to be parsimonious with the water for fear that if too much is applied at one time it will drain through and harm the surface underneath. This simply won't work because plants like to be watered well, not in dribbles, and if the plant survives long enough, inevitably you will over-water and perhaps not be aware of it until you discover a hole rotted in the Bigelow or an ugly mark on the parquet.

All of this reminds me to caution about unglazed clay saucers. Moisture seeps through them the same as it does the walls of an unglazed clay pot. In time this seepage will mar the surface on which it rests. You can avoid this problem but cutting a piece of half-inch cork to fit under each clay saucer; moisture dissipates through the cork and prevents moisture damage.

What about hanging containers? I use a little of everything, except no wire baskets in my apartment—they are sure to drip water in the wrong places. Most of my hanging plants grow in ordinary white plastic containers which come with wire hangers, but are suspended now in macrame or hand-thrown pottery. I hang them from ceiling hooks placed directly in front of, and slightly to the side, of the windows. To vary the heights I use small metal chains. If you are careful about watering hanging baskets, excess drainage should be a problem only occasionally. The secret is to keep the soil always in a range between slightly moist and *nicely* moist. If the soil dries out severely, it will draw away from the walls of the hanging container and, when water is applied it will run right through, overflowing the drainage saucer and causing a minor flood. The only way to avoid overwatering plants hung overhead is to reach up with your finger and touch the soil to feel if it is wet, moist, or dry. If you water one of these strictly by guessing, eventually, you are likely to drown it, or let it dry too much.

One of the most puzzling aspects of container gardening to beginners is what size pot each plant needs. It's nothing to worry about. In fact, before you have grown many plants you will begin to have a natural sense of whether a plant is in the right size pot or not. Just use common sense. In other words, if a plant looks top-heavy, as if it might topple over at the slightest disturbance, it probably needs a size or two larger pot. If a little plant looks lost in the pot, it is probably overpotted and would do better in a smaller size.

The rule of thumb I follow when it comes time to decide what size pot a plant needs is this: Measure the height of the plant; select a pot one-third to one-half this measurement. In other words, a busy-corn plant (*Dracaena fragrans*) 24 inches tall will do well in a pot eight to 12 inches in diameter. Plants that grow mostly in a horizontal plane instead of upright, such as African violet and Iron Cross begonia, can be measured across, from the tip of one leaf to one on the opposite side. An African violet nine inches across is likely to do well and look right in a three- to five-inch pot.

This rule of thumb doesn't work for tree-size house plants. Obviously, you don't see six-foot ficus trees growing in pots two or three feet in diameter. It's a generality, but six-foot trees usually do well in containers 12–15 inches in diameter; eight-foot trees in containers 15–18 inches across.

Potting plants is truly the easiest thing in the world, and yet the way people gather around to watch and ask questions when I demonstrate this aspect of plant growing, I gather it is an awesome task if you've never done it—or seen someone do it. Almost always your aim is to put the plant in a size or two larger pot than the one in which it has been growing—and to situate it in the new container at approximately the same level it grew in the old one. This means if you are moving a plant from a five- to six-inch pot, you will have to add approximately an inch of new potting soil in the bottom before you position the plant. Then you fill in all around the existing ball of soil and roots with fresh potting soil. If the roots are coiled around and around the old soil, or if they have formed a tight, meashlike covering, I gently uncoil some of them, or use a sharp knife to cut some shallow slashes in the old root-soil mass, to encourage the roots to grow into the new soil.

What about adding a layer of drainage first? I'll tell you a secret. I never add pebbles, broken pieces of clay flowerpot, screen wire or anything else over the bottom of the pot if it has a drainage hole. If it doesn't, I do add a layer of drainage which I discussed earlier in this chapter. If you've grown accustomed to adding a little drainage material in the bottom of pots before proceeding with the transplanting, I am not saying you should stop. I am just being truthful about the way I do it. Sometimes if the pot has a sizable drainage hole and I am using a fine-textured growing medium, such as one of the soil-less mixes discussed in Chapter 6, I tear off a piece of newspaper just to cover the hole and keep the growing medium in the pot until it has been well moistened. Otherwise, I'm lazy.

You'll have better luck with potting and repotting if you use a growing medium that is nicely moist at the beginning. Use your hands, a kitchen spoon or trowel to add the soil to the pot. Firm it gently but firmly into the pot so that no air pockets will be left around the roots. Then water well

Fold a sheet of newspaper into several thicknesses and use it to hold the cactus and protect your hands from the thorns; separate the plant and its soil from the old pot.
Bill Mulligan

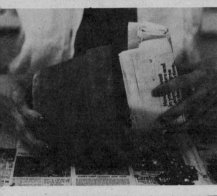

Repotting a thorny cactus requires caution. Tap the edge of the pot to release the soil.
Bill Mulligan

Now you can examine the soil and see whether or not roots have filled it; in this case none is visible, so repotting into the same pot is in order.
Bill Mulligan

and allow to drain before placing in the growing area. If the plant shows any signs of wilting, keep it out of direct sunlight for a few days. In severe cases where wilting continues, or many leaves begin to turn yellow, it may help to enclose the plant in clear plastic and keep it in bright light but no sun until signs of transplant shock disappear.

POTS AND POTTING TIPS. New clay pots, or those which have not been used recently, need to be soaked in a pail of water for an hour or two before you plant in them. Otherwise the dry clay will absorb too much water from the soil.

You'll be a more successful indoor gardener if you use only clean pots at transplanting time. I scrub mine in the kitchen sink, using an old pot scrubber, soap pads, a stiff toothbrush—even a wire brush for stubborn stains and encrustations—and then I rinse them in clean water. If I have no immediate need for the pots, I allow them to dry, then store for future use. Sometimes when I have a quantity of pots to clean I rinse them first in the sink and then fill up the dishwasher and run them through an entire cycle (but without detergent). Before you do this with a quantity of plastic pots, try one or two first along with the dishes just to be sure the dishwasher isn't going to melt them.

Plants need to be repotted when they fill with roots the container and soil in which they are growing. For how to check, see the section entitled "Size of the Plant" in Chapter 5. Seedlings, rooted cuttings and new division of house plants often need repotting to larger containers every two or three months for the first year. Older plants can get by on once-a-year repotting and large bushes and trees may do well for two years or more. What I like to do for a plant in a large container is scratch away the top two or three inches of soil in the inbetween years and replace it with fresh. If you do this, I recommend that you work only with your fingers so that the roots will be damaged as little as possible.

What about the white encrustation that forms on clay pots and sometimes even on plastic? This is a buildup of mineral salts from the water, the soil and fertilizer. It is more unsightly than it is harmful. Take the pot to your kitchen sink and use a stiff brush to remove the crusty salts; scrape off stubborn spots with the tip of a knife blade.

Incidentally, if you should receive a foil-wrapped gift plant, the first thing to do is remove the foil. It not only distracts from the natural beauty of the plant, but may prevent excess moisture from escaping through the drainage hole.

8. How to Bring a Baby Plant into the World

Plant parenthood helps satisfy the nurturing instinct in all of us. In most books about plants, you'll find this activity listed under propagation, which is perfectly correct, but only to a point. Sprouting a seed, rooting a cutting, or dividing a plant is only the beginning. If the young sprout is to grow up a healthy, well-adjusted adult, it's the after care that requires a real commitment to parenting.

Although this chapter is about basic plant propagation techniques, I hope you'll realize this is not as clinical as it sounds. Growing your own baby plants is an immensely satisfying and exciting experience. As you nurture your progeny through the early traumas of forming roots, and then withstanding transplanting shock, you will find your-self more involved with plants than you could have thought was possible.

Besides the fun of starting your own plants, another reason is to save money. You can grow a whole collection of different house plants from seeds and cuttings for what you might pay for a single large specimen. A recent experience I had illustrates the rewards of plant propagation.

One June day I was walking home from my office and just as I turned north on Madison Avenue at 56th Street, I saw a piece of coleus lying on the sidewalk. I hurried on, but by the time I reached 57th both my nurturing instinct and my desire for a good plant cheap had taken control. I turned around and retraced my steps, hoping what was about to become my cutting of a coleus unlike any I had at home had not been trampled underfoot. Fortunately, as I stooped to pick it up, I saw that only one leaf had been crushed. I took that slightly wilted foundling to my apartment, removed the bottom two leaves and placed the stem in a glass of water in bright light but no direct sun. One week later roots had formed and the cutting was ready to be transplanted to a pot of soil. That was six months ago and now I have two large specimen coleus plants from the original cutting and several smaller ones.

HOW TO START SEEDS. If your generation went to nursery school and kindergarten, you must surely have planted bean or corn seeds against the sides of a glass filled with moist soil and watched roots grow down and leaves grow up. And if you're old enough, as I am, not to have been sent to school before you had played away at least your first five or six years, by now you must surely have a notion of what happens when a seed sprouts. In other words, don't worry about basic botany—just plant some seeds and see what happens.

Most house plants can be grown from seeds, but finding

the kinds you want may require sending away to specialists (for addresses, see Chapter 11). Two plants whose seeds you'll find in most local seed racks include coleus and basil. Coincidentally, both are members of the Mint family, both are herbs in the broadest sense (coleus is an orna-

Lord & Burnham

Drawing shows technique for starting seeds such as coleus and basil; from top, pots, sterile planting medium, bulb mister, packets of seeds, allowing the planted pot to soak up moisture, the planted pot covered with plastic and finally the pot filled with seedlings, ready to be transplanted.

Author

It is vital that sprouting seeds and baby seedlings never dry out; uncover the container daily and feel the surface with your fingers; if it feels dry, add drops of water from a spoon, or use a bulb mister.

mental herb, and you know about basil), both have seeds of similar size, and both require similar treatment. Since neither is difficult to sprout nor to transplant, I suggest you purchase a packet of each.

Besides the seeds, you will need two six-inch pots, and one quart *each* of pasteurized all-purpose potting soil and vermiculite.

(1) Mix the soil and vermiculite together.

(2) Fill each of the pots to one-half inch from the top.

(3) Firm and smooth off with your fingers or the bottom of a drinking glass so that the finished surface is about one inch from the top of the pot.

(4) Open one of the packets and empty the seeds into the cupped palm of one hand; with the fingers of your other hand, pick up some of the seeds and sprinkle them

A few weeks after transplanting, your coleus seedlings will look like these.

These basil seedlings are off to a healthy start; pinching back can begin at this stage (see text).

Here is how to take a tip cutting from a cane-stemmed begonia.

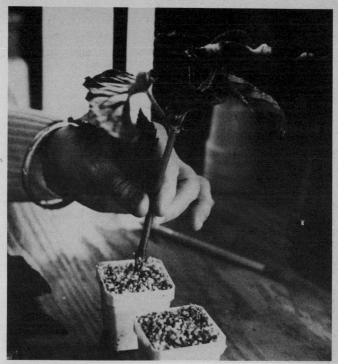

Remove the lower leaves from the cutting, and insert about 1½ inches of the stem in a pot of moist, sterile rooting medium; vermiculite is being used here.

over the soil surface; continue until all of the seeds are gone, distributing them as evenly as possible.

Repeat steps 1–4 for the other packet of seeds and pot of soil.

(5) Place some of the soil and vermiculite mixture in an ordinary kitchen sieve and sprinkle a slight single layer over the seeds you have just planted.

(6) Press the surface gently with the tips of your fingers.

(7) Set each pot in a bowl to which you have added two inches of tepid water; leave to soak until beads of moisture show on the surface; remove and allow to drain.

(8) After a half hour or so place a piece of glass over the top of the pot, or enclose the entire pot in a plastic bag.

(9) Set the pots where temperatures would be comfortable for you to sit and read, and in bright light but little or no direct sun.

(10) When you see the first sprouts, possibly in less than a week's time, remove the covering daily for an hour or two and touch the soil surface with your fingers to be sure it is moist; if it feels dry, add tepid water, either from a tablespoon or bulb sprayer.

(11) As soon as several green sprouts show, remove the covering entirely and place the pot in a sunny east, south, or west window. Until the seedlings grow enough for their leaves to begin to touch each other, all you have to do is be sure that the soil *never* dries out; try to keep it always nicely moist. This is vital to seedlings because they have shallow roots which will be killed if the surface soil dries out.

When the leaves of the seedlings touch and begin to crowd each other, it is time to transplant them to individual pots. For this you will need as many 2½- or three-inch pots as you have seedlings, and enough growing medium to fill them (mix two parts of all-purpose potting soil to one part of vermiculite).

(1) Add enough of the potting mix to each pot so that about an inch of space is left at the top.

(2) Use a kitchen fork to lift each seedling, bringing with it as many roots as possible.

(3) Position each seedling in the pot, holding it with one hand so that as you add potting mix around it with

It is important to remove the leaves from any part of the stem which will touch either soil or water; here wax begonia cuttings have been stripped of lower leaves and placed to root in a glass of water.

Author

your other hand it will stand at approximately the same level in the soil as it did before.

(4) Gently firm the soil in place around each seedling.

(5) When all have been transplanted, group the individual pots in a waterproof tray about two inches deep; add a little more than an inch of tepid water to the tray; this will be absorbed by the transplants.

(6) Keep the seedlings out of direct sunlight for a day or two until the leaves all stand erect, which indicates that the roots are settling in, then you can return the transplants to the same exposure where they were growing

before. From now on your seedlings will need the same care as if they were more mature plants of the same kind. Both coleus and basil respond to frequent pinching back which is explained in Chapter 9.

Once you are successful in starting easy plants like coleus and basil from seeds, you will be ready to try other kinds. If the seeds are dust-sized, as are those of African violet, gloxinia, and begonia, simply scatter them over the surface of the planting medium, but do not sift any over them; just enclose the pot in plastic or cover the top with a piece of glass. Larger seeds may be covered with a sifting of soil equal in thickness to their own diameter. Most house plant seeds need constant temperatures around 70 degrees and pasteurized soil that is never allowed to dry out during the time it takes for them to sprout and in the first few weeks afterwards while they are developing a healthy root system. For how to start an avocado pit (the

Here is how to plant a leaf cutting of African violet. Clear drinking glass acts as a mini-greenhouse.

In a few weeks or months clusters of baby plants will grow around the base of each parent African violet leaf. Separate and remove each, as shown.

Transplant each plantlet from the African violet leaf into an individual pot of moist soil.

In six months to one year's time, the plantlet on the left will grow to the size of the plant on the right.

Author

When a plant has several stems, crowns or rosettes of leaves arising from the soil as this African violet does, usually it can be divided.

93

equivalent of a seed in other house plants), see Chapter 10.

HOW TO START CUTTINGS. There are numerous, fascinating ways to start houseplants from cuttings, but if you start with a simple tip cutting of coleus and a leaf cutting of African violet, you will be well on your way to succeeding with more difficult plants.

To make a tip cutting of coleus, take a sharp paring knife and cut through a healthy stem just below where two full-size leaves are growing, and at a point so that the cutting will be three or four inches long. Remove the two lowermost leaves. You can root this cutting in a small glass of water (just be sure that none of the leaves is immersed). Or, you can plant the cutting directly in a pot of soil (mix together equal parts pasteurized all-purpose potting soil and vermiculite) with about an inch of the stem inserted in the soil and firmed in place with your fingers.

To root the cutting in water, simply place it in bright light but little or no direct sun, and be sure to maintain the water level. When roots are about an inch long, transplant to the same soil mix as for planting a cutting without roots. Moisten well. If the leaves wilt and fail to perk up after a few hours, turn a drinking glass over it to form a miniature greenhouse. As soon as the leaves look perky, remove the cover if you found one necessary, and place the cutting in a sunny exposure or bright north light. Future care will be the same as for more mature plants of the same type.

To make a leaf cutting of an African violet, select a healthy, mature leaf and break or cut it from the plant. Cut the leaf stem so that it is about one inch long. Insert this all the way up to where it joins the leaf in a pot of pasteurized growing medium (mix together equal parts all-purpose potting soil and vermiculite). Moisten well. Enclose pot and all in a plastic bag and place in a pleas-

Use a knife to cut the divisions apart, retaining as many roots as possible with each new plant.

This African violet yielded three divisions (the one on the left unfortunately has only a few roots, but with pampering it will take hold).

antly warm, bright place, but not in more than an hour of direct sun per day. Check the soil once a week; if it feels dry, add water. After a few weeks or a couple of months begin to look for baby plants coming up around the base of the leaf. When these are an inch or more high you can unpot the rooted leaf and divide the plants; occasionally

Author

The kitchen sink makes a good place to pot small plants, but it pays to put the plug in the drain first. Here a kitchen spoon is being used to add fresh potting soil around the roots of the African violet division.

a leaf will yield only one baby, but most African violets produce several. Other plants you can multiply from leaf cuttings are discussed in Chapter 10.

HOW TO DIVIDE HOUSE PLANTS. When a potted plant has more than one stem or rosette of leaves that emerges directly from the soil, it is a likely subject for removing from the pot and breaking apart, which is usually referred to as dividing. African violets with more than one rosette or crown of leaves emerging from the soil can be divided, as can be some spider plants, asparagus-ferns, wax begonias, and marantas (prayer plants). Transplant each division into a clean pot of fresh potting mix and take care to keep them always nicely moist and in bright light but little or no direct sun until old growth shows no signs of wilting. Then you can place them in the same amount of sun as the original plant was receiving.

You can also divide a plant without removing it from the soil. Simply take a kitchen knife and slice down into the soil between the stems, carefully severing the new plant from the old. Lift it out to be potted separately. Add enough fresh soil to the pot of the old plant to replace that taken with the new one.

Another plant propagation technique you can have fun with is air-layering, discussed in Chapter 10 under the entry for *Dracaena*.

9. Listen to Your Plants

Talk to your plants, sing to them, play beautiful music—whatever makes you feel like a good plant parent—but never neglect listening to what they may be saying to you in their own sign language. Plants communicate most often by:

A. Leaf drop
B. Leaf discoloration
C. Wilted leaves, stems or flowers
D. Spindly or malformed growth
E. Damaged growth
F. Mold, fungus, or otherwise sickly growth

Each of these signs may indicate a single problem or a combination of several. With a little practice you can accurately interpret what your plants are saying to you and thus become your own resident house plant doctor.

A. *Leaf drop*. This symptom may indicate:

(1) Change of environment
(2) Bone-dry soil
(3) Muddy, wet soil
(4) Too much fertilizer
(5) Insect or disease attack
(6) Too hot or too cold environment
(7) Lack of fresh air
(8) An atmosphere that is too dry
(9) Lack of light or sun
(10) Old age

And here is what you can do:

(1) Check needs of plant in good reference book. Try to duplicate as nearly as possible in your home. In time, plant should adapt.

(2) Be careful not to let soil dry out severely between waterings.

(3) Apply less water. Don't leave pot standing in saucer of water for more than an hour or two after watering. If container has no drainage hole and soil is muddy wet, remove plant and wash soil from roots; re-pot in fresh, moist soil, first adding an inch or two of pebbles and charcoal chips in the bottom. Water sparingly in the future so that soil feels moist to your fingers, not dripping wet.

(4) Drench soil with clean water to flush out excess fertilizer. Feed less in the future.

(5) See sections E and F, which follow.

(6) Check needs of plant in a good reference book; use maximum/minimum thermometer to determine tem-

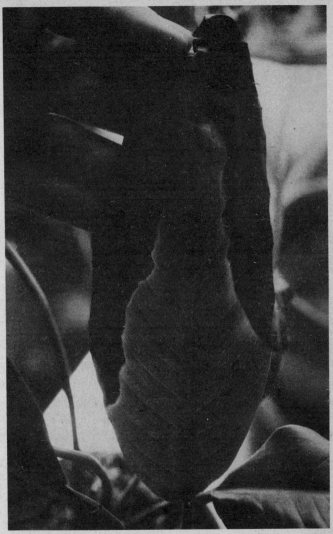

Maddy Miller

To learn what may have caused the blackened, dead portions seen on this spathiphyllum leaf, see Section B of the text.

101

perature range where plant is growing; adjust accordingly.

(7) Open window daily, only a crack in cold weather, more on warm days. Use oscillating fan to keep air circulating.

(8) Mist plants daily with water. Group pots on pebble trays kept nearly full of water. Use a cool-vapor humidifier.

(9) Move plant to more light or sun, or provide supplementary fluorescent or incandescent light.

(10) Natural; pick or cut from plant and discard.

B. *Leaf discoloration.* This symptom may indicate:

   (1) Change of environment
   (2) Bone-dry soil
   (3) Muddy, wet soil
   (4) Too much or not enough fertilizer
   (5) Lack of soil acidity
   (6) Too hot or too cold environment
   (7) Hot or cold drafts of air
   (8) Atmosphere too dry
   (9) Insect or disease attack
  (10) Mechanical damage

And here is what you can do:

(1–3) See section A, solutions 1–3.

(4) See section A, solution 4. Also, if you have not been feeding plant, begin applying a house plant fertilizer according to directions on the label; if a foliage plant, use all-purpose house plant fertilizer; if a flowering plant, apply African-violet or blooming-plant fertilizer.

(5) If reference books tell you the plant in question needs an acid soil, leaves that are yellowed or anemic-looking probably indicate the need for an acid-type fertilizer (available from a garden center; Mir-Acid is excellent). Often a problem with gardenia, azalea, and dwarf citrus such as calamondin.

(6) See section A, solution 6.

(7) Check to be sure plant is not placed where drafts of hot or cold air blow directly on it.

(8) See section A, solution 8.

(9) See sections E and F, which follow.

Author

For what may have caused this coleus stem to turn brown and rot, see Sections C and D.

(10) Plants recently purchased may have had leaves or stems bruised or broken in handling. Use scissors to trim off discolored parts of leaves.

C. *Wilted leaves, stems, or flowers.* These symptoms may indicate:

    (1) Bone-dry soil
    (2) Muddy, wet soil
    (3) Too much fertilizer
    (4) Too hot or too cold

(5) Hot or cold drafts of air

(6) Atmosphere too dry

(7) Insect or disease attack

(8) Mechanical damage

(9) Old age

And here is what you can do:

(1) See section A, solution 2; if soil dries out too rapidly and requires water more often than you have time to provide it, transplanting to a size or two larger pot is probably the answer.

(2) See section A, solution 3.

(3) See section A, solution 4.

(4) See section B, solution 6.

(5) See section B, solution 7.

(6) See section A, solution 8.

(7) See sections E and F, which follow.

(8) See section B, solution 10. Also, individual stems or leaves may have been broken in handling, the result being that only that part of the plant will be wilted; cut and remove broken parts; if piece of stem several inches long has been broken, it may perk up and sprout roots if placed in a glass of water. Healthy leaves of African violet, gloxinia, and rhizomatous begonias broken off in handling may also be used as cuttings.

(9) Natural for flowers past their prime; pick or cut from plant and discard.

D. *Spindly or malformed growth.* These symptoms may indicate:

Why have most of the leaves of this Chinese evergreen turned yellow and drooped dejectedly? See Section C of the text.

Author

104

(1) Lack of light or sun
(2) Too much direct sun
(3) Poorly drained soil
(4) Lack of fertilizer
(5) Too hot or too cold environment
(6) Atmosphere too dry
(7) Insect or disease attack
(8) Lack of fresh air
(9) Old age

And here is what you can do:

(1) See section A, solution 9.

(2) Check needs of plant in a good reference book; move accordingly to less direct sun.

(3) Remove plant from container. Work carefully with your hands to remove as much of the old soil as possible without breaking roots; wash off remaining soil in tepid water. Repot in fresh soil to which drainage material has been added; for example, mix together two parts (by volume) all-purpose packaged potting soil to one part *each* of peat moss, perlite, and vermiculite.

(4) Begin applying a house plant fertilizer according to directions on the label; if a foliage plant, use all-purpose house plant fertilizer; if a flowering plant, apply an African-violet or blooming-plant fertilizer.

(5) See section A, solution 6.

(6) See section A, solution 8.

(7) See sections E and F, which follow.

(8) See section A, solution 7.

(9) Old stems of some plants grow woody with age, coleus and Swedish-ivy in particular; start new tip cut-

Do you understand the sign language of this kalanchoe? See Section D of the text.

Author

Author

Why is this wax begonia reaching all in one direction? See Section D of the text.

Author

Does this African violet have a halo, or is something wrong? Find the answer in Section B of the text.

To learn what these bugs are and what to do about them, read Section E, number 5 in the text.

See Section E, solution 4, for an explanation of what is being done to this Ficus triangularis.

tings and discard old plant. Piggyback plant is relatively short-lived; when old plant begins to look scraggly, start new cuttings.

E. *Damaged growth.* This symptom may indicate:

(1) Aphids (greenish insects, usually clustered on now growth)

(2) Cyclamen mites (not visible to the naked eye; malformed new growth; most likely to attack African violets and cyclamen)

(3) Mealybugs (one-eighth-inch oblong insects with many legs, under leaves and on stems; visible cottony white residue)

(4) Red spider-mites (not readily visible; yellow or gray flecking of leaves; tiny webs between leaves and stems)

(5) Scale (one-eighth-inch oblong insects, tan, brown, black, or white)

(6) Thrips ($\frac{1}{16}$-inch long, black, threadlike insects; thin, papery scars visible on leaves and flowers; often attack gloxinias)

(7) White flies (small white flies clustered under leaves; they fly around when disturbed)

And here is what you can do:

(1) Wash off all aphids visible in tepid water; repeat at five-day intervals until eradicated. Or spray with synthetic pyrethrin; some growers find that a Shell No-Pest Strip placed in the room where plants are grown will control aphids. Misting plants every week or two with water to which Ced-o-flora or Dr. Bronner's Peppermint Soap has been added (follow directions on label for mixing proportions) will discourage aphids.

(2) Spray or dip plant alternately at weekly intervals with Kelthane and Dimite (both are miticides). Some

Author

For what is wrong with this gloxinia leaf, see Section E, item 6 in the text.

growers find that a Shell No-Pest Strip placed near cy-
clamen-mite-infested plants will solve the problem.

(3) Follow directions for aphids (item 1 above);
mealybugs are more persistent and require constant vigi-
lance to eradicate completely.

(4) Presence of red spider-mites indicates the air is
too stale, hot, and dry. To control, improve atmosphere;
also, wash plant repeatedly in tepid water to which Ced-
o-flora or Dr. Bronner's Peppermint Soap has been added
(see item 1 above). Controls suggested for cyclamen mites
(see item 2 above) may also be used.

(5) Remove with tip of knife blade, or treat as aphids
(item 1 above).

(6) Treat as aphilds (item 1 above).

(7) Treat as aphids (item 1 above).

F. *Mold, fungus, or sickly growth*. These symptoms
may include:

(1) White or grayish mold or encrustation on soil
surface, rim, and sides of pot (especially clay)

(2) White or grayish, threadlike filaments on dying
or dead leaves, stems, and flowers

(3) Plant collapses and falls over

(4) White or grayish, powdery spots on otherwise
healthy leaves

(5) White or yellow rings or spots on leaves, especially African violet, columnea, or other gesneriad

(6) Yellow, black, or brown spots on otherwise
healthy leaves And here is what you can do:

(1) An accumulation of mineral salts from soil, water,
and fertilizer is the cause. Skim off from soil surface with
spoon; cultivate lightly with kitchen fork. Use stiff brush
or soap pad to remove encrustation from pot rim and
sides; rinse in clean water.

(2) Remove all dying or dead leaves, stems, and flowers. In the future, promptly remove yellowing, dying growth as soon as you see it.

(3) Roots or stems have rotted from overwatering or

Author

What these insects (somewhat enlarged) are and what to do about them is explained in Section E, number 3 of the text.

overfeeding. Try to salvage cuttings of healthy tip growth; discard old soil and dead plant parts.

(4) Powdery mildew, a disease; frequent problem with begonias, especially Rieger, rex, angel-wing, and tuberous-rooted. Spray or dust with fungicide (ferbam or sulfur, for example, available where garden supplies are sold). Improve air circulation around plants.

(5) Caused by applying ice-cold water to soil or splashing it on the leaves. Use only water of room temperature or *slightly* warmer.

(6) Sunburned spots caused by too much hot sun

shining directly on the leaves; also caused when plants grow too tall in a fluorescent-light garden and touch the tubes, or from placing an incandescent plant light too close to the foliage.

OTHER PROBLEMS. Plants that grow rapidly such as coleus, Swedish-ivy, and wandering Jew need to have the growing tips removed frequently. This procedure is

Author

For why this African violet has malformed new growth in the center, see Section E, number 2 in the text.

called pinching back and it causes the plant to form many branches instead of one tall or long spindly one. What you do is nip or pinch out the tip of the stem along with the uppermost pair of leaves. Usually two new branches will begin to grow just below where you pinched off the tip of the original main stem. When the new branches are about two inches long, pinch out the tip of each. Soon you will have four branches, then eight, 16, and so on.

If you have an older plant such as coleus, Swedish-ivy, or wandering Jew with very long, ungainly or spindly stems, you may need to cut or pinch off more than just the tip. For example, if you have a single-stem coleus 18 inches tall, it may be a good idea to cut it back to six inches. Use the part you cut off to make one or two tip cuttings. The same is true of a hanging basket of Swedish-ivy or wandering Jew which has a few long, ungainly stems with most of the leaves at the bottom and very few around the sides of the basket. Nipping out the ends of these will result only in more growth at the bottom and none at the top where you want it. Again, the best procedure is to cut back drastically and use as many of the cut-off pieces as tip cuttings as you want to.

Climbing philodendrons are often sold with a piece of rough bark or tree-fern in the pot on which the plant stems have been trained. Whether bark or tree-fern, this is called a totem pole, and it is intended to provide for the plant a rough, moist surface on which it can climb, the same as if it were growing wild in the tropics where it would likely climb on a tree trunk. The problem with the commercial product is that usually the plant has already neared the top of the totem pole, and shortly after you bring it home it runs out of a place on which to climb. Future growth will produce under-sized leaves and, in the case of split-leaf philodendron, the characteristic splitting will disappear entirely and the new leaves will appear to be of a different variety.

If you have such a plant, you can simply cut off the stems when they reach the top of the totem, thus encouraging the plant to sprout new growth further down which will then have a rough surface on which to climb by means of its aerial roots. Or, you can move the plant to a

This spotted-leaf angelwing begonia seems to have developed two foreign spots. For what they are and what to do about them, see Section 5, number 4 in the text.

size larger pot, at the same time adding a taller totem attached to the back of the one on which the plant is growing already. To help new growth, tie it to the totem with strips of dark green plastic, and mist the totem surface with water several times a week so that it will be moist enough to attract the aerial roots. In my opinion, philodendrons which need a totem pole on which to climb are not ideal house plants; you can do better with several hundred other kinds.

10. 101 House Plants with a Strong Will to Live

Deciding which plants to include in this chapter has not been easy. In fact, it is largely arbitrary, because once the specific needs of a plant are clearly outlined, as they are here, almost anything is possible. However, I have chosen to omit from the list some of the most common house plants simply because they are difficult, and responsible for a major number of the questions I receive. These include asparagus-fern, schefflera, cutleaf philodendron, zebra-plant, gardenia, and geranium. My reasons for omitting these are:

Asparagus-fern. This plant is highly susceptible to red spider-mite infestation and also mealybugs. If the soil

Pots of any florist-grown plant like these daffodils and tulips will last longer indoors if the soil is kept always moist, if they are protected from drafts of hot, dry air, and if they receive bright light but little or no sun shining directly on the petals.

dries out severely even once, it will drop hundreds of leaflets or needles all over the floor. However, if you can provide a temperature range of 60–70°F during the winter heating season, with plenty of freely circulating fresh air and constantly moist soil, asparagus-fern can be a never-say-die house plant.

Schefflera. Very temperamental about soil moisture; if too dry, older leaves turn yellow and fall off; if too wet, new growth develops black tips and dies. Schefflera is also so much used in commercial decorating that if I see it in a living room, I feel as if I am paying a visit to my bank. Schefflera's relative, the *Trevesia,* makes a much better house plant and it is far from being common.

Cutleaf philodendron. Like Schefflera, this plant is too commercial for me to want to grow it at home, and besides, unless the climbing stems have a moist, rough surface on which to attach themselves, new growth will be spindly and unattractive. I have included other philodendrons which are not only interesting but good investments as house plants.

Zebra-plant. Aphelandra, otherwise known as zebra-plant, grows like a weed in commercial greenhouses where the atmosphere is always moist and the soil *never* dries out, not even slightly. But the minute you bring it home, trouble begins. Slight drying of the soil causes *all* of the older leaves to die and fall off. Red spider-mites love zebra-plant. Many other plants with similarly attractive variegated foliage are more easily grown.

Gardenia. Buy one of these with an open, fragrant flower or two and covered with buds, and you're almost certainly asking for trouble. The gardenia has exacting needs as to temperature and humidity, not to mention a decided preference for acid soil. The changes of environment from commercial greenhouse to local plant shop to your home are enough to guarantee that all developing flower buds will dry up and die, unopened. Keeping the plant alive, on the other hand, is not all that difficult. *Never* let the soil dry out, give it a place in a sunny east, south, or west window with temperatures in a range of 60–72°F, mist the leaves daily, and feed with an acid-type fertilizer according to directions on the container. If you are absolutely faithful to the gardenia's needs, it may thrive for you, develop new flower buds, and actually bloom.

Geranium. To omit this plant from my list is like saying I hate apple pie, but it's the truth, geraniums do not make good plants in the average house or apartment. They need full sun in the winter, temperatures no higher than 70°F and moist soil—never wet, never dry. Furthermore, a geranium that blooms outdoors all summer on your terrace or in a window box cannot be expected to continue blooming all winter. The only geraniums I find worth growing as all-year house plants are the scented-leaf types, especially apple (sometimes called all-spice), lemon, and rose.

Other plants I have not included in my list of 101 die-hards include the seasonal flowering types, usually acquired from a florist and given or received as a gift. These are azalea, chrysanthemum, cyclamen, poinsettia, fancy-leaved caladium, calceolaria (pocketbook plant), cineraria, Christmas cherry and Christmas pepper, hydrangea, tulip, daffodil, hyacinth, crocus, and paperwhite narcissus. While these are in bloom, the best care you can give them is to keep the soil *always* nicely moist in a place where there is bright light but where hot sun does not shine directly on the flowers; drafts of hot, dry air, or temperatures above 72°F shorten the life of the flowers. I am not saying you shouldn't buy these plants, what I am saying is that you should not expect them to become permanent residents. I consider my investment in a season-

Acorus calamus variegatus, *miniature sweet flag.*

ing flowering plant the same as buying fresh cut flowers. While it lasts, enjoy the beauty; when the flowers are gone and the foliage ceases to be attractive, discard the plant.

Two of my own favorite plants I have not included in this chapter are amaryllis and gloxinia. Both grow from bulbs, and both are easy foliage plants, but getting them to bloom again after the initial crop is not easy. If you have an amaryllis, treat it as *Agapanthus* or *Clivia* (both included in this chapter); gloxinias need more sun than African violets, but otherwise care is similar (see *Saintpaulia*).

To understand the environmental needs as outlined for the plants in this chapter, study Chapters 1–9, 12–13.

Acorus

PRONUNCIATION: ACK-or-us
COMMON NAME: Sweet flag and miniature sweet flag.
USES. Desktop, sill, or terrarium.
LEAF COLOR: Green or green and white.
FLOWERS: No.

Environmental Needs
LIGHT: Bright light to two hours sun; thrives in a fluorescent-light garden.
TEMPERATURE: 62–72°F.
HUMIDITY: Medium to high.
MIST FREQUENTLY: Yes.
SOIL MIX: African violet or terrarium.
SOIL MOISTURE: Between moist and wet.
PROPAGATION: By division.
PROBLEMS: Dry soil and hot, dry air cause leaf tips to die; subject to red spider-mite attack.

Adromischus

PRONUNCIATION: ad-ROH-mish-us
COMMON NAME: Plover eggs; calico hearts.
USES: Desktop, sill, or open terrarium.
LEAF COLOR: Green, silver, purple.
FLOWERS: No.

Environmental Needs
LIGHT: Sunny east, south, or west window.
TEMPERATURE: 62–75°F.
HUMIDITY: Low.
MIST FREQUENTLY: No.
SOIL MIX: Cactus.
SOIL MOISTURE: Between moist and on the dry side.
PROPAGATION: By division.
PROBLEMS: If chilled and wet at the same time, roots
   may rot.
COMMENTS: These are succulent plants which are
   able to withstand underwatering.

Aechmea

PRONUNCIATION: ECK-me-uh
COMMON NAME: Bromeliad.
USES: Desktop, wide sill, hanging basket, or pedestal.
LEAF COLOR: Green, burgundy, silver.
FLOWERS: Pink, red, blue.

Environmental Needs
LIGHT: Sunny east, south, or west window; tolerates
   bright light without direct sun indefinitely if mature
   to begin with; thrives in a fluorescent-light garden.
TEMPERATURE: 62–75°F.
HUMIDITY: Medium; tolerates less.
MIST FREQUENTLY: Yes.
SOIL MIX: Cactus.
SOIL MOISTURE: Evenly moist to nearly dry; once
   a week, fill cup formed by leaves with clean water,
   but pour out old water before adding fresh.
PROPAGATION: By division, usually a few months
   after the plant has flowered.
PROBLEMS: None, unless roots stand in water for
   long periods of time, in which case the roots may rot.

Jackson & Perkins

'Silver King' aechmea, a bromeliad, as silvery green leaves and rose and blue flowers contained by a showy, long-lasting bract of pink.

COMMENTS: "Silver King" aechmea is the most popular bromeliad sold by local florists and plant shops; other aechmeas, available from specialists (see Chapter 11), are also showy and easy to grow.

Aeschynanthus

PRONUNCIATION: esk-uh-NANTH-us

COMMON NAME: Lipstick vine.

USES: Hanging basket or pedestal.

LEAF COLOR: Green; less common *A. marmoratus* has yellowish green and burgundy variegation.

FLOWERS: Red.

Environmental Needs

LIGHT: Sunny east or west window; tolerates bright light without direct sun, but may not flower.

TEMPERATURE: 62–75°F.

HUMIDITY: Medium to high; tolerates less.

MIST FREQUENTLY: Yes.

SOIL MIX: African violet or terrarium.

SOIL MOISTURE: Evenly moist; tolerates some dryness.

PROPAGATION: Tip cuttings in any season.

PROBLEMS: Mealybugs may attack.

COMMENTS: Lipstick vine is an unusually carefree basket or pedestal plant because the stems do not require pinching back; new growth, which sprouts from the base, keeps the plant full and compact in appearance.

African violet: See **Saintpaulia**

Agapanthus

PRONUNCIATION: ag-uh-PANTH-us

COMMON NAME: Lily-of-the-Nile.

USES: Desktop, sill, floor plant, or pedestal.

LEAF COLOR: Green.

FLOWERS: Blue or white.

Environmental Needs

LIGHT: Sunny east, south, or west window.

TEMPERATURE: 60–72°F.

HUMIDITY: Medium.

MIST FREQUENTLY: Yes, if convenient.
SOIL MIX: All-purpose.
SOIL MOISTURE: Evenly moist.
PROPAGATION: By division.
PROBLEMS: Virtually trouble-free. Soil allowed to become severely dry will cause older leaves to turn yellow and die, but the resumption of regular watering promotes rapid new growth.
COMMENTS: Agapanthus grows from a bulb and is common as an outdoor plant in frost-free climates. Elsewhere you may have to send away for it to specialists; for addresses, see Chapter 11.

Agave

PRONUNCIATION: uh-GAH-vee
COMMON NAME: Century plant.

Author

Closeup of a basket of aeschynanthus or lipstick vine in bloom.

128

Agapanthus grow like this outdoors all year in warm-weather climates, but you will find it also makes an excellent plant for a sizable pot or tub indoors.

USES: Desktop, sill, or pedestal.
LEAF COLOR: Green, blue-green, creamy white.
FLOWERS: Rarely.

Environmental Needs
LIGHT: Sunny east, south, or west window; young agaves grow well in a fluorescent-light garden.
TEMPERATURE: 62–75°F.
HUMIDITY: Low.
MIST FREQUENTLY: No.
SOIL MIX: Cactus.
SOIL MOISTURE: Evenly moist to on the dry side.
PROPAGATION: By division.

PROBLEMS: If chilled and wet at the same time, agave roots may rot.

COMMENTS: These succulent plants tolerate periods of considerable dryness without harm.

Aglaonema

PRONUNCIATION: ag-loh-NEE-muh

COMMON NAME: Chinese evergreen.

USES: Desktop, sill, or terrarium; a large specimen aglaonema may be used for tree effect if displayed on a tall pedestal.

LEAF COLOR: Green, silver, white, yellow, pink.

FLOWERS: White, similar to a calla lily, followed by berries, at first green, then red.

Environmental Needs

LIGHT: Bright, but little or no direct sun; young aglaonemas thrive in a fluorescent-light garden.

TEMPERATURE: 62–75°F.

HUMIDITY: Low to medium.

MIST FREQUENTLY: Yes, if convenient.

SOIL MIX: All-purpose or African violet.

SOIL MOISTURE: Between nicely moist and wet.

PROPAGATION: Tip cuttings in any season.

PROBLEMS: Trouble-free.

COMMENTS: Aglaonema is one of the best of all foliage plants to cultivate in low-light areas; it will thrive in an office where the only light received is from ceiling fluorescents.

Airplane plant: See Chlorophytum

Aloe

PRONUNCIATION: al-OH-ee

COMMON NAME: *A. vera* is sometimes called medicine or unguentine plant.

USES: Desktop, sill, hanging basket, or pedestal.
LEAF COLOR: Green, blue-green, sometimes variegated with white or silver.
FLOWERS: Rarely.

Environmental Needs
LIGHT: Sunny east, south, or west window; small aloes will thrive in a fluorescent-light garden.
TEMPERATURE: 62–75°F.
HUMIDITY: Low.
MIST FREQUENTLY: No.
SOIL MIX: Cactus.
SOIL MOISTURE: Between evenly moist and on the dry side.
PROPAGATION: By division.
PROBLEMS: If chilled and wet at the same time, aloe roots may rot.
COMMENTS: These succulent plants tolerate underwatering and neglect.

Aluminum plant: See **Pilea**

Ananas

PRONUNCIATION: uh-NAN-us
COMMON NAME: Pineapple; bromeliad.
USES: Desktop, sill, hanging basket, or terrarium.
LEAF COLOR: Gray-green, or green variegated with creamy white to yellow and rose-red.
FLOWERS: Mature plants produce a pineapple (edible), crowned by a rosette of leaves.

Environmental Needs
LIGHT: Sunny east, south, or west window; tolerates bright light without direct sun indefinitely if mature to begin with; thrives in a fluorescent-light garden.
TEMPERATURE: 62–75°F.

131

Hort-Pix

You may have seen Agave americana marginata *growing to this giant size outdoors in warm climates, but it also makes an excellent house plant when young.*

HUMIDITY: Medium; tolerates less.

MIST FREQUENTLY: Yes.

SOIL MIX: Cactus.

SOIL MOISTURE: Evenly moist to nearly dry; once a week, fill cup formed by leaves with clean water, but pour out old water before adding fresh.

PROPAGATION: When the pineapple fruit begins to shrivel (or before if you plan to eat it), remove the new rosette on top with about a half-inch of the fruit attached; set aside to dry overnight, then plant with base in soil mix and keep in a range between evenly moist and nearly dry.

PROBLEMS: None, unless roots stand in water for long periods of time, in which case they may rot.

132

COMMENTS: You can root the top cut from a commercial pineapple in the same way as described above for the ornamental types.

Aporocactus

PRONUNCIATION: uh-por-oh-KACK-tus
COMMON NAME: *A. flagelliformis* is known as rat-tail cactus.
USES: Hanging basket or pedestal.
LEAF COLOR: Green.
FLOWERS: Red.

Environmental Needs
LIGHT: Sunny east, south, or west window.
TEMPERATURE: 62–75°F.
HUMIDITY: Low.
MIST FREQUENTLY: Not necessary.
SOIL MIX: Cactus.
SOIL MOISTURE: Between nicely moist and nearly dry.
PROPAGATION: Tip cuttings, ideally in spring or summer.
PROBLEMS: Mealybugs may attack; if chilled and wet at the same time, roots may rot.
COMMENTS: This cactus makes a durable hanging basket or pedestal plant in full sun and tolerates considerable watering neglect.

Aralia: See Fatsia

Aralia: See Polyscias

Aralia, false: See Dizygotheca

Araucaria

PRONUNCIATION: are-oh-KAY-ree-uh

Plain Chinese evergreen, an aglaonema, thrives in low- to bright-light areas, but needs no hot sun shining directly on its leaves.

Author

'Silver King' aglaonema or Chinese evergreen has bright green leaves heavily variegated with silver.

COMMON NAME: *A. excelsa* is the Norfolk Island pine.

USES: Desktop, sill, or terrarium while young; eventually becomes a tree.

FLOWERS; No.

Environmental Needs

LIGHT: Sunny east or west window; tolerates more or less light if other conditions are favorable.

TEMPERATURE: 62–75°F during the winter heating season.

The Herb Grower Magazine

Aloe vera *is one of the easiest of all house plants to grow.*

HUMIDITY: Medium; tolerates less.
MIST FREQUENTLY: Yes.
SOIL MIX: All-purpose or African violet.
SOIL MOISTURE: Evenly moist.
PROPAGATION: From tip cutting, but difficult.
PROBLEMS: Severely dry soil will cause many needles
 or branches to die, if not the entire plant. Avoid

Author

Araucaria or Norfolk Island pine about two feet tall.

Author

Ardisia or coralberry bears a long-lasting crop of bright red berries.

138

Aspidistra will thrive in low-light areas where almost nothing else would grow, except possibly Chinese evergreen (aglaonema) and sansevieria.

drafts of hot, dry air in winter. Red spider-mite may attack in stale, hot air.

Ardisia

PRONUNCIATION: are-DEEZ-ee-uh
COMMON NAME: Coralberry.
USES: Desktop, sill, or terrarium while young; older ardisias may be used as floor shrubs or hanging basket plants.
LEAF COLOR: Green.
FLOWERS: Pinkish white, followed by green berries which turn shiny red and last for several months.

Environmental Needs

LIGHT: Sunny east, south, or west window; young ardisias grow well in a fluorescent-light garden.

TEMPERATURE: 62–75°F.

HUMIDITY: Medium.

MIST FREQUENTLY: Yes, if convenient.

SOIL MIX: All-purpose or African violet.

SOIL MOISTURE: Evenly moist.

PROPAGATION: Tip cuttings, ideally in spring or summer.

PROBLEMS: Resents drafts of hot, dry air, especially in combination with dry soil, but remarkably care-free.

Areca palm: See **Chrysalidocarpus**

Artillery fern: See **Pilea**

Aspidistra

PRONUNCIATION: ass-puh-DIST-ruh

COMMON NAME: Cast-iron plant.

USES: Floor shrub or pedestal.

LEAF COLOR: Green or green-and-white variegated.

FLOWERS: Yes, but insignificant.

Environmental Needs

LIGHT: Bright to low light, but little or no direct sun.

TEMPERATURE: 62–75°F.

HUMIDITY: Low to medium.

MIST FREQUENTLY: Yes, but only if convenient.

SOIL MIX: All-purpose or African violet.

SOIL MOISTURE: Evenly moist to on the dry side.

PROPAGATION: By division.

PROBLEMS: None.

COMMENTS: Aspidistra is one of the best of all plants to grow in areas of low light; thrives in an office where ceiling fluorescents provide the only illumination.

Avocado: See **Persea**

Baby's-tears: See **Helxine**

Basil: See **Ocimum**

Bay, sweet: See **Laurus**

Beaucarnea

PRONUNCIATION: boh-KARN-ee-uh
COMMON NAME: Ponytail; elephant's-foot.
USES. Desktop or sill while young; older plants may be used as floor shrubs, for tree effect, in a hanging basket, or displayed on a pedestal.
LEAF COLOR: Green.
FLOWERS: No.

Environmental Needs
LIGHT: Sunny east, south, or west window; tolerates bright light with little or no direct sun; young beaucarneas will thrive in a fluorescent-light garden.
TEMPERATURE: 62–75°F.
HUMIDITY: Low.
MIST FREQUENTLY: No.
SOIL MIX: Cactus or all-purpose.
SOIL MOISTURE: Evenly moist to nearly dry.
PROPAGATION: Occasionally by division.
PROBLEMS: If chilled and wet at the same time, the roots may rot.
COMMENTS: Beaucarnea forms a large bulblike growth which stores moisture; tolerates underwatering for long periods of time, especially older specimens.

Begonia

PRONUNCIATION: be-GOH-nee-uh
COMMON NAME: Begonia.
USES: Desktop, sill, floor shrub, hanging basket, pedestal, or terrarium.
LEAF COLOR: Green, silver, red, yellow.

Jun Yamakawa

Beaucarnea, the ponytail or elephant-foot plant.

142

Author

Wax or semperflorens begonias are among the easiest of all flowering plants to grow indoors.

FLOWERS: White, pink, rose, red, orange.

Environmental Needs
LIGHT: Sunny east or west window; most do well near a sunny south window in winter. Small kinds thrive in fluorescent-light gardens.

TEMPERATURE: 62–75°F.

HUMIDITY: Low to medium.

MIST FREQUENTLY: No.

SOIL MIX: All-purpose, African violet, or terrarium.

SOIL MOISTURE: Evenly moist.

PROPAGATION: Tip cuttings, leaf cuttings (if rex or rhizomatous type), division.

PROBLEMS: Overfeeding may cause a begonia to collapse and die; wet, poorly drained soil may cause root and stem rot.

COMMENTS: Easiest begonias to grow are the wax or *semperflorens,* rhizomatous (sometimes called beefsteak or star begonias) and angelwing or cane types. The glorious flowering Rieger hybrids sold by florists are difficult to maintain as house plants except in a temperature range of 55–65°F during the winter heating season.

Billbergia

PRONUNCIATION: bill-BERJ-ee-uh

COMMON NAME: Queen's-tears; bromeliad.

USES: Desktop, sill, hanging basket, or pedestal.

LEAF COLOR: Green, silver, burgundy.

FLOWERS: Red, green, blue, violet, pink, yellow.

Environmental Needs

LIGHT: Sunny east, south, or west window; tolerates bright without direct sun indefinitely if mature to begin with; thrives in a fluorescent-light garden.

TEMPERATURE: 62–75°F.

HUMIDITY: Medium to high; tolerates less.

MIST FREQUENTLY: Yes.

SOIL MIX: Cactus.

SOIL MOISTURE: Evenly moist to nearly dry; once a week, fill cup formed by leaves with clean water, but pour out old water before adding fresh.

Rhizomatous, star or beefsteak begonias are good choices for a beginner. This one is growing in the bright light of a north-facing apartment window in New York City.

Author

This silver-spotted angelwing begonia grows approximately 12 inches away from a sunny east window.

PROPAGATION: By division, usually a few months after the plant has flowered.

PROBLEMS: None, unless roots stand in water for long periods of time, in which case the roots may rot.

COMMENTS: Many showy and easy-to-grow billbergias are available from specialists (see Chapter 11).

Bird-of-paradise: See **Strelitzia**

Boston fern: See **Nephrolepis**

Bromeliad: See **Aechmea, Ananas, Billbergia, Cryptanthus, Neoregelia, Vriesea**

Burro's-tail: See **Sedum**

Cactus: See **Aporocactus, Cephalocereus, Cereus, Echinocactus, Echinocereus, Echinopsis, Gymnocalycium, Lemaireocereus, Lobivia, Mammillaria, Opuntia, Schlumbergera**

Calamondin: See **Citrus**

Calathea

> PRONUNCIATION: kal-uh-THEE-uh; kuh-LAY-thee-uh
>
> COMMON NAME: Calathea.
>
> USES: Desktop, sill, hanging basket, pedestal, or terrarium.
>
> LEAF COLOR: Green, silver, burgundy.
>
> FLOWERS: No.
>
> *Environmental Needs*
>
> LIGHT: Bright light or an hour or two of direct sun; thrives in a fluorescent-light garden; sometimes seen in office gardens where the only light received is from ceiling fluorescents.
>
> TEMPERATURE: 62–75°F.
>
> HUMIDITY: Medium to high, but tolerates less.
>
> MIST FREQUENTLY: Yes.
>
> SOIL MIX: African violet or terrarium.
>
> PROPAGATION: By division.
>
> PROBLEMS: Drafts of hot, dry air, especially in combination with dry soil, may cause leaf tips to die.
>
> COMMENTS: Calatheas are beautiful foliage plants, related to the more common maranta or prayer plant, but somewhat less prone to leaf tip browning.

Calico hearts: See **Adromischus**

Callisia

> PRONUNCIATION: kuh-LISS-ee-uh
>
> COMMON NAME: None, but *C. elegans* is sometimes referred to as *Setcreasea striata*.
>
> USES: Desktop, sill, hanging basket, or pedestal.
>
> LEAF COLOR: Green, white, and purple.

Maddy Miller

Calathea makes a beautiful foliage plant with leaves that are relatively resistant to dieback.

Author

Carludovica, the Panama hat plant, resembles a palm and is easily cultivated.

148

FLOWERS: Insignificant.

Environmental Needs

LIGHT: Sunny east, south, or west window; thrives in a fluorescent-light garden.

TEMPERATURE: 62–75°F.

HUMIDITY: Medium.

MIST FREQUENTLY: Yes, if convenient.

SOIL MIX: All-purpose.

SOIL MOISTURE: Evenly moist.

PROPAGATION: Tip cuttings.

PROBLEMS: If leaves wilt from severely dry soil, most of the tips will turn brown.

Candelabra plant: See Euphorbia

Carludovica

PRONUNCIATION: kar-loo-DOH-vick-uh

COMMON NAME: Panama hat plant.

USES: Floor shrub; tree effect if placed on a pedestal.

LEAF COLOR: Green.

FLOWERS: No.

Environmental Needs

LIGHT: Bright light or a few feet back from a sunny window.

TEMPERATURE: 62–75°F.

HUMIDITY: Medium.

MIST FREQUENTLY: Yes, if convenient.

SOIL MIX: All-purpose.

SOIL MOISTURE: Evenly moist.

PROPAGATION: Division.

PROBLEMS: Drafts of hot, dry air, especially in combination with dry soil, may cause the leaf tips to die. If this happens, trim off the dead parts with a pair of scissors, and try to avoid letting the soil dry out in the future.

This young cereus cactus gives no hint that one day, with abundant sunlight and warmth, it may be nearly 12 inches in diameter and several feet tall.

COMMENTS: This plant is closely related to and appears to be a palm. It is an outstanding house plant, but not easily found in local shops; available by mail from Alberts & Merkel (see Chapter 11).

Caryota

PRONUNCIATION: kay-ree-OH-tuh

COMMON NAME: *C. mitis* is the fishtail palm.
USES: Floor shrub or tree effect.
LEAF COLOR: Green.
FLOWERS: No.

Environmental Needs
LIGHT: Bright light or a few feet back from a sunny
   window.

Richard Fish/Hort-Pix
Chamaedorea elegans is an ideal small plant for the beginner.

TEMPERATURE: 62–75°F.
HUMIDITY: Low to medium.
MIST FREQUENTLY: Yes, if convenient.
SOIL MIX: All-purpose.
SOIL MOISTURE: Evenly moist to wet.
PROPAGATION: Division.
PROBLEMS: In hot, dry, stale air, red spider-mite may attack.

Cast-iron plant: See **Aspidistra**

Century plant: See **Agave**

Cephalocereus

PRONUNCIATION: suh-fal-oh-SEER-ee-us
COMMON NAME: *C. senilis* is the old man cactus.
USES: Desktop, sill, or pedestal plant.
LEAF COLOR: Gray-green, completely covered by long white hairs.
FLOWERS: Rarely as a house plant.

Environmental Needs
LIGHT: Sunny east, south, or west window.
TEMPERATURE: 62–75°F.
HUMIDITY: Low.
MIST FREQUENTLY: No.
SOIL MIX: Cactus.
SOIL MOISTURE: Evenly moist to nearly dry.
PROPAGATION: By division if offsets form around base of old plant.
PROBLEMS: Wet soil in combination with cold temperatures may cause the roots to rot.

Cereus

PRONUNCIATION: SEER-ee-us
COMMON NAME: Cereus.

USES: Desktop or sill while young; older plants may be used as floor shrubs or for tree effect; sometimes striking when displayed on a pedestal as a piece of sculpture.

LEAF COLOR: Green or gray-green.

FLOWERS: Night-blooming and white.

Environmental Needs

LIGHT: Sunny east, south, or west window.

TEMPERATURE: 62–75°F.

HUMIDITY: Low.

MIST FREQUENTLY: No.

SOIL MIX: Cactus.

SOIL MOISTURE: Evenly moist to nearly dry.

PROPAGATION: By removing offsets that form around the base of an older plant and treating as cuttings.

PROBLEMS: Wet, poorly drained soil in combination with poor light and chilly temperatures may result in root rot.

COMMENTS: These are mostly column-forming cacti, sometimes growing as a single column, sometimes branched or clustered.

Ceropegia

PRONUNCIATION: seer-oh-PEE-jee-uh

COMMON NAME: Rosary vine; hearts entangled.

USES: Hanging basket or pedestal.

LEAF COLOR: Green and silver.

FLOWERS: Greenish and purple-brown.

Environmental Needs

Light, sunny east, south, or west window; tolerates bright light with little or no direct sun.

TEMPERATURE: 62–75°F.

HUMIDITY: Low.

Rohm and Haas

Chlorophytum, the spider plant, displayed on a tall, narrow shelf unit of Plexiglas.

MIST FREQUENTLY: No.

SOIL MIX: Cactus or all-purpose.

SOIL MOISTURE: Evenly moist to on the dry side.

PROPAGATION: Stem cuttings mature enough to have formed bulblike growths.

PROBLEMS: Virtually none; a good plant for beginners.

Cestrum

PRONUNCIATION: SESS-trum

COMMON NAME: *C. nocturnum* is sometimes called night jessamine.

USES: Desktop, sill, floor shrub, hanging basket, or pedestal.

LEAF COLOR: Green.

FLOWERS: White, usually in summer, and intensely fragrant at night.

Environmental Needs

LIGHT: Sunny east, south, or west window.

TEMPERATURE: 62–75°F.

HUMIDITY: Medium.

MIST FREQUENTLY: Yes, if convenient.

SOIL MIX: All-purpose or African violet.

SOIL MOISTURE: Evenly moist.

PROPAGATION: Tip cuttings, ideally in spring or summer.

PROBLEMS: If soil dries out severely, to the point that the leaves wilt, most of the older ones will die.

COMMENTS: This plant is seldom found in local shops, but it is available from mail-order specialists (see Chapter 11).

Chamaedorea

PRONUNCIATION: kam-uh-DOH-ree-uh

COMMON NAME: Dwarf palm.

USES: Desktop, sill, floor shrub, pedestal (if large, a pedestal-displayed chamaedorea may give the effect of a tree); fine for terrarium or bottle garden while young.

LEAF COLOR: Green.

FLOWERS: Insignificant.

Environmental Needs

LIGHT: Bright light or an hour or two of direct sun.

TEMPERATURE: 62–75°F.

HUMIDITY: Medium; tolerates less.
MIST FREQUENTLY: Yes, if convenient.
SOIL MIX: All-purpose.
SOIL MOISTURE: Evenly moist.
PROPAGATION: Division if multistemmed.

Hort-Pix

Chrysalidocarpus lutescens, *usually called the areca palm.*

PROBLEMS: Red spider-mite may attack if the atmosphere is hot, dry, and stale. Dry soil in combination with too much heat will cause tips of the fronds to die.

COMMENTS: *Chamaedorea elegans* may eventually grow to six feet high; its variety *bella,* sometimes called *Neanthe bella,* grows only two or three feet high.

Chamaerops

PRONUNCIATION: KAM-uh-rops

COMMON NAME: *C. humilis* is the European fan palm.

USES: Floor shrub, for tree effect, or display on a pedestal.

LEAF COLOR: Green.

FLOWERS: No.

Environmental Needs

LIGHT: Sunny east, south, or west window.

TEMPERATURE: 62–72°F.

HUMIDITY: Medium.

MIST FREQUENTLY: Yes, if convenient.

SOIL MIX: All-purpose.

SOIL MOISTURE: Evenly moist.

PROPAGATION: Division if multistemmed.

PROBLEMS: Red spider-mite may attack if the atmosphere is hot, dry, and stale. Dry soil in combination with too much heat will cause tips of the fronds to die.

Chinese evergreen: See Aglaonema

Chlorophytum

PRONUNCIATION: kloh-roh-FYE-tum

COMMON NAME: Spider plant; airplane plant.

USES: Desktop, sill, hanging basket, or pedestal.
LEAF COLOR: Green or green and white.
FLOWERS: White, but insignificant.

Environmental Needs
LIGHT: Bright light or near a sunny east, west, or
   south window; young plants of common spider plant
   and all sizes of miniature *c. bichettii* will thrive in a
   fluorescent-light garden.
TEMPERATURE: 62–75°F.
HUMIDITY: Medium, tolerates less.
MIST FREQUENTLY: Yes, if convenient.
SOIL MIX: All-purpose.
SOIL MOISTURE: Evenly moist.
PROPAGATION: Division or remove and plant the
   babies which form on the runners.
PROBLEMS: If the soil dries out severely, older leaves
   will die entirely and the tips of others will turn brown.
COMMENTS: Opinions vary as to why common spi-
   der plant fails on occasion to send out runners with
   baby plants; some authorities say the plant has to first
   fill the pot with roots, others say that too much artificial light at night delays or prevents runner growth.

Christmas cactus: See Schlumbergera

Chrysalidocarpus

   PRONUNCIATION: kriss-al-id-oh-KARP-us
   COMMON NAME: Butterfly palm; areca palm.
   USES: Floor shrub or tree.
   LEAF COLOR: Green.
   FLOWERS: No.

   Environmental Needs
   LIGHT: Near a sunny east, south, or west window;

158

keeps fairly well without direct sun, but may need supplementary fluorescent or incandescent light.

TEMPERATURE: 62–75°F.

HUMIDITY: Medium.

MIST FREQUENTLY: Yes, if convenient.

SOIL MIX: All-purpose.

SOIL MOISTURE: Evenly moist to wet.

PROPAGATION: By division, but difficult.

PROBLEMS: Red spider-mites may attack if air is hot, dry, and stale. Severely dry soil will cause leaf tips to die and turn brown.

COMMENTS: This palm is more graceful than the kentia (howeia) and far less expensive, but not as easily cultivated indoors. The two major causes for failure with it are red spider-mites and allowing the soil to become too dry between waterings.

Cissus

PRONUNCIATION: SISS-us

COMMON NAME: Grape-ivy; kangaroo vine.

USES: Desktop, sill, hanging basket, pedestal.

LEAF COLOR: Green.

FLOWERS: No.

Environmental Needs

LIGHT: Near a sunny east, south, or west window; adapts to bright light with little or no sun shining directly on the leaves; does well in fluorescent-light gardens, or with supplementary light from an incandescent floodlight.

TEMPERATURE: 62–72°F during the winter heating season.

HUMIDITY: Medium; tolerates less.

MIST FREQUENTLY: Yes, if convenient.

SOIL MIX: All-purpose.

Citris mitis *or calamondin, a miniature orange*.

SOIL MOISTURE: Evenly moist to on the dry side.

PROPAGATION: Stem cuttings of fairly mature growth.

PROBLEMS: Red spider-mites are likely to attack in air that is hot, dry and stale. Wet, poorly drained soil may cause leaf drop. Soil allowed to become severely dry will result in most of the older leaves turning brown and dying almost immediately, as well as the tender new growth.

COMMENTS: Grape-ivy (*Cissus rhombifolia*) and kangaroo vine (*C. antarctica*) are among the best of all hanging baskets plants, but take care not to hang them near the ceiling in a hot room, or directly over a radiator in winter.

Citrus

PRONUNCIATION: SIT-truss

COMMON NAME: Lemon, lime, orange, grape-fruit, calamondin, tangerine.

USES: Desktop, sill, floor shrub, pedestal (for tree effect).

LEAF COLOR : Green.

FLOWERS: White and fragrant.

Environmental Needs

LIGHT: Sunny east, south, or west window, seedlings thrive in fluorescent-light garden.

TEMPERATURE: 62–72°F during the winter heating season.

HUMIDITY: Medium.

MIST FREQUENTLY: Yes, if convenient.

SOIL MIX: African violet or terrarium.

SOIL MOISTURE: Evenly moist to on the dry side.

PROPAGATION: Seeds (easy) or cuttings (difficult).

PROBLEMS: Citrus needs acid soil; if the soil becomes too alkaline ("sweet"), leaves will develop yellowish mottling; correct by feeding with acid-type fertilizer, available wherever gardening supplies are sold. Mealybugs and white citrus scale may attack. If air is hot, dry and stale, red spider-mites may invade. If soil dries out severely, many leaves will die and fall from the plant almost overnight.

COMMENTS: Seeds taken from a ripe citrus fruit sprout readily when planted one-fourth-inch deep in moist soil. They become handsome foliage plants, but seldom flower. Dwarf citrus plants sold by florists and by mail from specialists (see Chapter 11. for addresses) are better choices if you want flowering fruiting plants.

Clivia

PRONUNCIATION: KLYE-vee-uh
COMMON NAME: Clivia or Kaffir lily.
USES: Floor or pedestal plant.
LEAF COLOR: Green.
FLOWERS: Apricot.

Environmental Needs
LIGHT: Bright light in or near a sunny east, south or west window; sun shining directly on the leaves for several hours a day is not necessary.
TEMPERATURE: 60–72°F.
HUMIDITY: Medium.
MIST FREQUENTLY: Yes, if convenient.
SOIL MIX: All-purpose.
SOIL MOISTURE: Evenly moist to on the dry side.
PROPAGATION: By division.
PROBLEMS: Virtually trouble-free. When clivia fills its pot with roots and has many strong leaves, keep constantly on the dry side and withhold fertilizer for two or three months; then resume feeding and watering and flowering should occur.
COMMENTS: Clivia makes a striking all-year foliage plant; the flowers are a beautiful bonus. Available from mail-order specialists; see Chapter 11 for addresses.

Author

Clivia is one plant that doesn't mind being slightly potbound; this one might well be transferred to a new pot one size larger any time within the next six months.

Clusia

PRONUNCIATION: KLEW-zee-uh
COMMON NAME: Clusia.
USES: Floor shrub or tree; place shrub size on pedestal for tree effect.

LEAF COLOR: Green or green and yellow.
FLOWERS: Rose-pink.

Environmental Needs
LIGHT: Near a sunny east, south, or west window.
TEMPERATURE: 62–75°F.
HUMIDITY: Medium.
MIST FREQUENTLY: Yes, if convenient.
SOIL MIX: All-purpose.
SOIL MOISTURE: Evenly moist.
PROPAGATION: By cuttings.
PROBLEMS: Red spider-mites are likely to attack if air is hot, dry, and stale; watch for mealybugs.
COMMENTS: An excellent, large-leaved indoor tree, still relatively difficult to find in local shops. It is available by mail from Alberts & Merkel (see Chapter 11 for address).

Coccoloba

PRONUNCIATION: koh-koh-LOH-buh
COMMON NAME: Sea-grape.
USES: Floor shrub or tree; place shrub size on pedestal for tree effect.
LEAF COLOR: Olive- to yellow-green; red veins.
FLOWERS: White, followed by purple fruit—but rarely indoors as a house plant.

Environmental Needs
LIGHT: Near a sunny east, south, or west window.
TEMPERATURE: 62–72°F during the winter heating season.
HUMIDITY: Medium.
MIST FREQUENTLY: Yes, if convenient.
SOIL MIX: All-purpose.
SOIL MOISTURE: Evenly moist.
PROPAGATION: By cuttings.

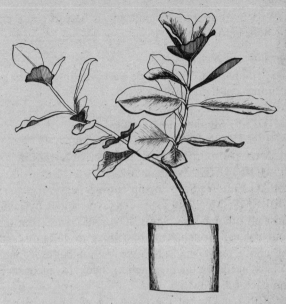

Jun Yamakawa

Clusia rosea, *an excellent indoor tree.*

PROBLEMS: Mealybugs often attack sea-grape; red spider-mites may invade if the air is hot, dry, and stale.

COMMENTS: An excellent house plant, but rarely seen in local Northern plant shops; available by mail from Alberts & Merkel (see Chapter 11 for address).

Coleus

PRONUNCIATION: KOH-lee-us
COMMON NAME: Coleus.
USES: Desktop, sill, hanging basket, pedestal.

LEAF COLOR: Green, chartreuse, red, pink, burgundy.

FLOWERS: Blue, but insignificant, is best to pinch off the buds before they develop.

Environmental Needs

LIGHT: Sunny east, south, or west window; thrives in a fluorescent-light garden.

TEMPERATURE: 62–75°F.

HUMIDITY: Medium; tolerates less.

MIST FREQUENTLY: Yes, if convenient.

SOIL MIX: All-purpose, African violet, or terrarium.

SOIL MOISTURE: Evenly moist.

PROPAGATION: Seeds or tip cuttings; easy.

PROBLEMS: Mealybugs seem to favor coleus over almost all other house plants; if you discover them on your coleus, probably the best thing to do is discard the entire plant and start over with a bug-free one. Coleus needs frequent pinching back to encourage compact, full growth.

COMMENTS: One of the easiest of all house plants, but after a year or two the old stems become woody and tend to produce inferior growth; it's best to start new plants annually from tip cuttings or seeds.

Coralberry: See **Ardisia**

Corn plant: See **Dracaena**

Crassula

PRONUNCIATION: KRASS-yew-luh

COMMON NAME: Jade plant; many other crassulas also make easy, rewarding house plants.

USES: Desktop, sill, floor shrub; place a large, old jade plant on a pedestal fot tree effect.

LEAF COLOR: Green, blue-green, gray.

166

FLOWERS: White or pink.

Environmental Needs

LIGHT: Sunny east, south, or west window; small
kinds or young plants do well in a fluorescent-light
garden.

TEMPERATURE: 62–72°F during the winter heating
season.

Keystone Products, Inc.

*A well-grown coleus makes a plant anyone would be proud
of, especially when displayed attractively as this one is in a
chrome planter.*

HUMIDITY: Low.
MIST FREQUENTLY: No.
SOIL MIX: All-purpose or cactus.
SOIL MOISTURE: Evenly moist to on the dry side in spring and summer; mostly on the dry side in fall and winter.
PROPAGATION: Tip or leaf cuttings.
PROBLEMS: Mealybugs often attack crassulas. Insufficient light causes spindly, anemic-looking growth. Wet, poorly drained soil is likely to result in rooted roots.
COMMENTS: If kept cool (50–65°F) and nearly dry in winter, jade plant is an excellent keeper in low light. However, a jade treated in the manner will need several months of recuperation in sun during warm weather, but move it gradually to more light so as not to sunburn the leaves.

Creeping Charlie: See Pilea

Crown of thorns: See Euphorbia

Cryptanthus

PRONUNCIATION: kripp-TANTH-us
COMMON NAME: Earth stars, a bromeliad.
USES: Desktop, sill, hanging basket or terrarium.
LEAF COLOR: Green, bronze, white pink.
FLOWERS: White.

Environmental Needs
LIGHT: Near a sunny east, south or west window; mature plants keep well almost indefinitely in bright light but little or no direct sun. Thrives in a fluorescent-light garden.
TEMPERATURE: 62–75°F.

Here the rounded, dark green leaves of jade plant (Crassula) *is surrounded by those of an* Agave *(larger, sword-shaped leaves) and an* Echeveria.

HUMIDITY: Medium to high, but tolerates less.

MIST FREQUENTLY: Yes, if convenient.

SOIL MIX: Terrarium or African violet.

SOIL MOISTURE: Evenly moist to on the dry side.

PROPAGATION: By removing offsets.

PROBLEMS: Pest-free and practically fail-safe. Constantly wet, poorly drained soil may cause the roots to rot.

COMMENTS: One of the easiest, most beautiful of all small colorful foliage plants. More unusual kinds not available in local shops may be ordered from specialists; see Chapter 11 for addresses.

Cycas

PRONUNCIATION: SIGH-kuss
COMMON NAME: Sago palm.
USES: Floor shrub or pedestal plant.
LEAF COLOR: Green.
FLOWERS: No.

Environmental Needs
LIGHT: Near a sunny east, south, or west window.
TEMPERTURE: 62–72°F during the winter heating
season.
HUMIDITY: Medium.
MIST FREQUENTLY: Yes.
SOIL MIX: All-purpose.
SOIL MOISTURE: Evenly moist to on the dry side; be
sure not to leave the pot standing in a saucer of water
in the fall and winter.
PROPAGATION: By removing offset from mature
plant, but difficult.
PROBLEMS: Red spider-mites may be troublesome if
the air is hot, dry, and stale. Neither constantly wet
nor severely dry soil is to the liking of cycas.
COMMENTS: Water somewhat less and apply no fertilizer unless your cycas is obviously sending up new
growth. Keep cycas away from radiators or other
sources of heat in the winter.

Cyperus

PRONUNCIATION: sigh-PEER-us
COMMON NAME: Umbrella plant.
USES: Desktop, sill, or pedestal.
LEAF COLOR: Green
FLOWERS: Greenish, but insignificant.

Author

Cryptanthus zonatus, *an earth-star bromeliad.*

Author

Cycas revoluta, *the Sago palm.*

171

Environmental Needs

LIGHT: Near a bright or sunny window, but sun shining directly on the leaves is not necessary.

TEMPERATURE: 62–72°F during the winter heating season.

HUMIDITY: Medium.

MIST FREQUENTLY: Yes.

SOIL MIX: All-purpose, African violet or terrarium.

SOIL MOISTURE: Evenly moist to wet.

PROPAGATION: By division.

PROBLEMS: Red spider-mites may attack if the atmosphere is hot, dry, and stale. If the soil dries out severely the leaf tips will turn brown and die.

COMMENTS: Cyperus is one of the few plants that don't mind standing in a saucer of water. Avoid placing it near any source of heat in the winter where hot air would blow directly on the leaves.

Cyrtomium

PRONUNCIATION: sir-TOH-mee-um

COMMON NAME: Holly fern.

USES: Desktop, sill, hanging basket, pedestal.

LEAF COLOR: Green.

FLOWERS: No.

Environmental Needs

LIGHT: Near a bright or sunny window, but sun shining directly on the leaves is not necessary; thrives in a fluorescent-light garden.

TEMPERATURE: 62–72°F during the winter heating season.

HUMIDITY: Medium; tolerates less if the soil is always nicely moist.

MIST FREQUENTLY: Yes, if convenient.

SOIL MIX: African violet or terrarium.

SOIL MOISTURE: Evenly moist.
PROPAGATION: By division.
PROBLEMS: Virtually trouble-free. If soil dries out severely, new growth may wither and die and old leaves may develop brown tips.
COMMENTS: Holly fern, especially the *Rochefordianum* variety of *Cyrtomium falcatum,* is one of the easiest of all ferns to grow as a house plant.

Davallia

PRONUNCIATION: duh-VAL-lee-uh
COMMON NAME: Rabbit's-foot fern.
USES: Desktop, sill, hanging basket, pedestal.
LEAF COLOR: Green.
FLOWERS: No.

Environmental Needs
LIGHT: Near a bright or sunny window, but sun shining directly on the leaves for more than an hour or two is not desirable.
TEMPERATURE: 62–75°F.
HUMIDITY: Medium.
MIST FREQUENTLY: Yes, if convenient.
SOIL MIX: African violet or terrarium.
SOIL MOISTURE: Evenly moist.
PROPAGATION: By rhizome cuttings.
PROBLEMS: Too much direct sun may cause new fronds to wither and die and older ones to develop brown leaflets; allowing the soil to dry out severely causes similar damage.
COMMENTS: Although davallia is delicate in appearance, it is actually one of the easiest of all ferns to grow as a house plant.

Devil's-ivy See Scindapsus

Dieffenbachia

PRONUNCIATION: deef-in-BOCK-ee-uh
COMMON NAME: Dumbcane.
USES: Floor shrub or tree effect.
LEAF COLOR: Green or green and cream.
FLOWERS: No.

Environmental Needs
LIGHT: Near a sunny east, south, or west window, but sun shining directly on the leaves for more than an hour or two is not necessary.
TEMPERATURE: 62–75°F.
HUMIDITY: Medium; tolerates less.
MIST FREQUENTLY: Yes, if convenient.
SOIL MIX: All-purpose.
SOIL MOISTURE: Evenly moist to on the dry side.

The beautiful frond of Davallia fegeensis, *the rabbit's-foot fern.*

Author

174

PROPAGATION: By stem cuttings or air-layering. To air-layer, use a knife to cut halfway through the stem at the point where you want roots to form. Wedge a piece of wooden toothpick or matchstick into the cut. Wrap a handful of well-moisted sphagnum moss around the stem, completely covering the cut part. Wrap the moss with a piece of polyethylene plastic, tying it securely top and bottom with strips of plastic or plant ties. Check weekly to be sure the moss is always moist; if it feels dry, moisten it well before replacing the plastic cover. When roots are growing vigorously into the moss, cut through the stem an inch or two below where the roots have formed. Pot up the new plant as described in Chapter 7. If you continue to get the bottom part of the old plant good care, it will send out new growth even though you may have removed all of its leaves as part of the new plant.

PROBLEMS: Red spider-mites are likely to attack if the air is hot, dry, and stale. If the soil dries out severely, older leaves are likely to turn yellow and die prematurely.

COMMENTS: The juice contained by all parts of the dieffenbachia are poisonous.

Dizygotheca

PRONUNCIATION: dizzy-GOTH-ick-uh
COMMON NAME: False aralia.
USES: Floor shrub or tree effect.
LEAF COLOR: Bronzy green.
FLOWERS: No.

Environmental Needs
LIGHT: Near a bright or sunny window, but sun shining directly on the leaves for more than an hour or two is not required.

175

Dieffenbachia or dumbcane as a young plant; in a year's time this one could reach nearly to ceiling height.

The young leaves of dizygotheca.

Dracaena fragrans massangeana, *a beautiful foliage plant that needs bright light but little or no sun shining directly on its leaves.*

177

Dracaena marginata,
the Madagascar dragon tree.

Author

TEMPERATURE: 62–75°F.
HUMIDITY: Medium; tolerates less.
MIST FREQUENTLY: Yes, if convenient.
SOIL MIX: All-purpose.
SOIL MOISTURE: Evenly moist.
PROPAGATION: Cuttings of partly mature stems.
PROBLEMS: Dizygotheca resents being moved around,
  even within the same room. When you bring one
  home, it is almost certain to lose a quantity of the
  older leaves, but if you give it thoughtful care, healthy
  growth should resume. Do not begin applying fertilizer
  until the plant has obviously made a satisfactory adjustment. Either soggy wet, poorly drained soil or
  severely dry soil will cause dizygotheca to shed leaves.

178

Dracaena

PRONUNCIATION: druh-SEE-nuh

COMMON NAME: Corn plant, Madagascar dragon tree.

USES: Desktop, sill, floor shrub, tree effect, or pedestal.

LEAF COLOR: Green, or green with white, yellow, red, silver, or pink.

FLOWERS: Small white and fragrant, but rarely.

Environmental Needs

LIGHT: Near a bright or sunny window, but sun shining directly on the leaves for more than an hour or two is not required.

TEMPERATURE: 62–75°F.

HUMIDITY: Medium; tolerates less.

MIST FREQUENTLY: Yes, if convenient.

SOIL MIX: All-purpose.

SOIL MOISTURE: Evenly moist to wet.

Author

Dracaena deremensis warneckei *has gray-green leaves striped with pure white.*

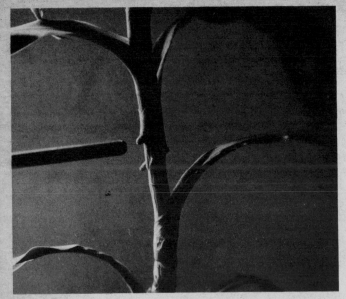

Air roots have already begun to grow on this dracaena stem—obviously a good place to make an air-layer.

PROPAGATION: Tip cuttings, division or by air-layering (for how-to, see *Dieffenbachia*).

PROBLEMS: Nearly trouble-free, but severely dry soil will cause the leaf tips to turn yellow or brown and die. *D. marginata* (Madagascar dragon tree) may drop quantities of the lower leaves if over- or under-watered.

COMMENTS: *D. fragrans* (corn plant) and its variegated form, *massangeana,* are two of the best of all plants for low-light areas, along with *D. deremensis warneckei* which has gray-green leaves distinctly striped with white.

Dumbcane: See Dieffenbachia

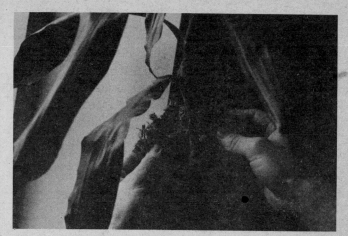

Wrap a handful of moistened unmilled spaghnum moss around where you want a new root system to form.

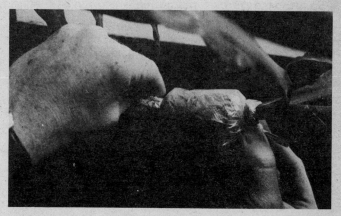

Wrap a piece of plastic around the moist moss and tie it securely at top and bottom. Be sure to add more water to the moss from time to time to maintain constant moisture. When roots fill the moss, cut through the stem just below where the roots are growing and pot up your new plant.

Earth stars: See **Cryptanthus**

Echeveria

PRONUNCIATION: eck-uh-VEER-ee-uh

COMMON NAME: Echeveria; a succulent.

USES: Desktop, sill, pedestal, or open terrarium.

LEAF COLOR: Green, blue-green, bronze, coppery pink.

FLOWERS: Red, yellow, orange, pink.

Environmental Needs

LIGHT: Sunny east, south, or west window; adapts well to a fluorescent-light garden.

TEMPERATURE: 62–75°F.

HUMIDITY: Low.

MIST FREQUENTLY: No.

SOIL MIX: All-purpose.

SOIL MOISTURE: Evenly moist to on the dry side; water somewhat less in fall and winter.

PROPAGATION: By division or leaf cuttings.

PROBLEMS: Watch for mealybugs. Wet, poorly drained soil is likely to result in rotted roots.

COMMENTS: These succulents grow mostly as low rosettes of thick, symmetrically arranged leaves with subtle and beautiful coloration; the seasonal flowers are simply an added bonus. Unusual kinds are available by mail from specialists; see Chapter 11 for addresses.

Echinocactus

PRONUNCIATION: eck-ee-noh-CACK-tus

COMMON NAME: *E. grusonii* is the handsome golden barrel cactus.

USES: Desktop, sill, or display on a pedestal as a piece of living sculpture.

LEAF COLOR: Green, but covered with golden spines.
FLOWERS: Yellow.

Environmental Needs
LIGHT: Sunny east, south, or west window.
TEMPERATURE: 62–75°F.
HUMIDITY: Low.
MIST FREQUENTLY: No.
SOIL MIX: Cactus.
SOIL MOISTURE: Evenly moist to on the dry side in spring and summer; mostly on the dry side in fall and winter.
PROPAGATION: By removing offsets.
PROBLEMS: Constantly wet, poorly drained soil is likely to cause root rot. Golden barrel, like most cactus, if allowed to dry out completely may die; if this should happen to your golden barrel, water very sparingly at first to give the roots time to readjust.
COMMENTS: Specimen plants of golden barrel, up to two feet in diameter, are fairly commonly available from local plant shops; smaller ones may be obtained by mail from specialists (see Chapter 11 for addresses).

Echinocereus

PRONUNCIATION: eck-een-oh-SEER-ee-us
COMMON NAME: A large grouping of small, cylindrical cacti, noteworthy for attractively arranged and colored spines and beautiful flowers.
USES: Desktop, sill, or open terrarium.
LEAF COLOR: Green, with spines of contrasting color.
FLOWERS: Pink, purple, red, orange, yellow.

Environmental Needs
LIGHT: Sunny east, south, or west window.

The beautiful blue-green leaf rosette of an echeveria.

TEMPERATURE: 62–75°F.

HUMIDITY: Low.

MIST FREQUENTLY: No.

SOIL MIX: Cactus.

SOIL MOISTURE: Evenly moist to on the dry side in spring and summer; mostly on the dry side in fall and winter.

PROPAGATION: By removing offsets.

PROBLEMS: Soggy wet, poorly drained soil will cause the roots to rot. Insufficient light will result in pale, undersized, malformed new growth.

COMMENTS: Many unusual echinocereus are available by mail from specialists; see Chapter 11 for addresses.

Echinopsis

PRONUNCIATION: eck-in-OPP-sis
COMMON NAME: *E. multiplex* is the Easter lily cactus.
USES: Desktop, sill, or open terrarium.

Echinocactus gruso-nii *has so many yellow spines it is called the golden barrel.*
Abbey Garden

LEAF COLOR: Shades of green with spines of contrasting color.
FLOWERS: White, pink, rose.

Environmental Needs
LIGHT: Sunny east, south, or west window.
TEMPERATURES: 62–75°F.
HUMIDITY: Low.
MIST FREQUENTLY: No.
SOIL MIX: Cactus.
SOIL MOISTURE: Evenly moist to on the dry side in spring and summer; mostly on the dry side in fall and winter.
PROPAGATION: By removing offsets.

Author

Eucharis is beautiful as a foliage plant all year, but when the white, fragrant, daffodil-like blooms open it is truly special.

PROBLEMS: Soil allowed to be severely dry or soggy wet for long periods of time may result in disintegration of the root system.

COMMENTS: Several different kinds of echinopsis are available by mail from specialists; see Chapter 11 for addresses.

Elephant bush: See **Portulacaria**

Elephant's-foot: See **Beaucarnea**

English ivy: See **Hedera**

Eucharis

PRONUNCIATION: YEW-kuh-riss
COMMON NAME: Eucharist lily.
USES: Desktop, wide sill, pedestal.
LEAF COLOR: Dark green.
FLOWERS: White, occasionally; fragrant.

Environmental Needs
LIGHT: Near a sunny east, south, or west window, but with little hot sun shining directly on the leaves.
TEMPERATURE: 62–72°F.
HUMIDITY: Medium; tolerates less.
MIST FREQUENTLY: Yes, if convenient.
SOIL MIX: All-purpose.
SOIL MOISTURE: Evenly moist; after plant has filled the pot with roots and has many leaves, keeping it on the dry side and withholding fertilizer for two months, then resuming normal watering and feeding should result in flower production.
PROPAGATION: By division.
PROBLEMS: Virtually trouble-free.
COMMENTS: Eucharis grows from a bulb; available from numerous mail-order firms (addresses in Chap-

This strange-appearing succulent is sometimes called brain cactus, but it is actually Euphorbia lactea cristata.

ter 11). The leaves resemble those of spathiphyllum, but they have a more leathery quality and are less prone to brown tips. An outstanding house plant.

Eucharist lily: See **Eucharis**

Euphorbia

PRONUNCIATION: yew-FOR-bee-uh

COMMON NAME: Crown of thorns (*E. milii* and varieties), pencil plant or milkbush (*E. tirucalli*), candelabra plant (*E. lactea*).

USES: Desktop, sill, floor shrub, for tree effect, or pedestal display.

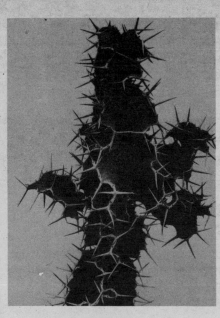

Euphorbia grandicornis *makes a stark appearance and may well be treated as a piece of living sculpture.*

Hort-Pix

LEAF COLOR: Green.

FLOWERS: Except for the poinsettia (see Comments, below) most euphorbias are cultivated as foliage plants.

Environmental Needs

LIGHT: Sunny east, south, or west window.

TEMPERATURE: 62–75°F.

HUMIDITY: Low.

MIST FREQUENTLY: No.

SOIL MIX: All- purpose.

SOIL MOISTURE: Evenly moist to on the dry side; be careful not to overwater in fall and winter.

PROPAGATION: By cuttings; set aside until the milky juice which flows from the cut stems dries, then plant.

PROBLEMS: Insufficient light will result in pale, undersized new growth. Virtually pest-free.

COMMENTS: With the exception of the Christmas poinsettia (*E. pulcherrima*), the succulent euphorbias mentioned above, and dozens of others available by mail from specialists (see Chapter 11 for addresses), make fascinating, trouble-free house plants.

Fatsia

PRONUNCIATION: FAT-see-uh
COMMON NAME: Aralia.
USES: Floor shrub, tree, or pedestal plant.
LEAF COLOR: Green.
FLOWERS: Yes, but insignificant.

Environmental Needs
LIGHT: Near a sunny east, south, or west window, but sun shining directly on the leaves for more than an hour or two is not desirable.
TEMPERATURE: 60–70°F during the winter heating season.
HUMIDITY: Medium.
MIST FREQUENTLY: Yes, if convenient.
SOIL MIX: All-purpose.
SOIL MOISTURE: Evenly moist.
PROPAGATION: Stem cuttings.
PROBLEMS: Red spider-mites may attack if the air is hot, dry, and stale; watch also for mealybugs. Avoid placing fatsia where drafts of hot air blow on it.
COMMENTS: An excellent large-leaved foliage plant for any bright room kept cool in the winter.

Fern: See Cyrtomium, Davallia, Nephrolepis, Platycerium, Polypodium

Ficus

PRONUNCIATION: FYE-kuss

Hort-Pix

Fatsia japonica *makes an excellent indoor shrub or tree, provided winter temperatures stay generally under 70 degrees F.*

COMMON NAME: Weeping fig *(F. benjamina),* rubber tree *(F. elastica),* Indian laurel *(F. retusa nitida),* fiddleleaf fig *(F. lyrata).*

USES: Floor shrub, tree, or pedestal plant.

Ficus lyrata, *the fiddleleaf fig, is an outstanding indoor tree.*

LEAF COLOR: Green.

FLOWERS: No.

Environmental Needs

LIGHT: Near a sunny east, south, or west window. Insufficient light causes leaf drop, but ficus respond well to supplementary artificial light.

TEMPERATURE: 62–75°F.

HUMIDITY: Medium; tolerates less.

MIST FREQUENTLY: Yes, if convenient.

SOIL MIX: All-purpose.

SOIL MOISTURE: Evenly moist.

PROPAGATION: Stem cuttings or by air-layering (for how-to, see *Dieffenbachia* in this chapter).

PROBLEMS: Red spider-mites may attack if the air is hot, dry and stale. If the soil dries out severely, many leaves will rapidly fall from ficus; if prolonged, entire branches may die. Too much hot sun shining directly on the leaves will cause yellow, brown, or black burned spots to form.

COMMENTS: Ficus are perhaps the best of all indoor plants where the effect of a leafy tree is desired.

Fig: See **Ficus**

Fishtail palm: See **Caryota**

Fittonia

PRONUNCIATION: fit-TOH-nee-uh

COMMON NAME: Nerve plant.

USES: Desktop, sill, hanging basket, pedestal, or terrarium.

LEAF COLOR: Green and white or green and rose-pink.

FLOWERS: White, but insignificant.

Environmental Needs

LIGHT: Bright, but little or no sun shining directly on the leaves is needed; grows to perfection in a fluorescent-light garden.

TEMPERATURE: 62–75°F.

193

Ficus elastica *'Decora,'* an improved variety of common rubber tree.

Hort-Pix

HUMIDITY: Medium.

MIST FREQUENTLY: Yes, if convenient.

SOIL MIX: African violet or terrarium.

SOIL MOISTURE: Evenly moist.

PROPAGATION: Tip cuttings.

PROBLEMS: Severely dry soil may cause older leaves to die and the tips of others to turn brown; however, fittonia is surprisingly tolerant of occasional dry soil to the point that leaves wilt slightly; it perks up soon after being watered and misted. Susceptible to root rot if planted in soggy wet, poorly drained soil.

COMMENTS: An unusually carefree and beautiful foliage plant, commonly available, but often overlooked because it appears to be delicate.

Flaming sword: See **Vriesea**

Fluffy ruffles fern: See **Nephrolepis**

Furcraea

PRONUNCIATION: FUR-kree-uh

COMMON NAME: Furcraea, a succulent member of the amaryllis family.

USES: Best displayed on a pedestal as a living piece of sculpture, and possibly to give the effect of a tree indoors.

LEAF COLOR: Green, blue-green, or green and white.

FLOWERS: No.

Environmental Needs

LIGHT: Near a sunny east, south, or west window.

TEMPERATURE: 62–72°F during the winter heating season.

HUMIDITY: Low.

MIST FREQUENTLY: No.

SOIL MIX: All-purpose.

SOIL MOISTURE: Evenly moist to on the dry side in spring and summer; mostly on the dry side in fall and winter.

PROPAGATION: By removal of offsets.

PROBLEMS: Virtually trouble-free, but dislikes soggy wet soil and hot, stale air in the winter.

COMMENTS: This succulent forms large rosettes of sword-shaped leaves and may remind you of certain agaves or yuccas. Seldom seen in local plant shops,

Ficus benjamina, *the weeping fig.*
Terrestris

This variegated-foliage form of Ficus elastica *(rubber tree) is just as easily grown as its parent.*

but small specimens are available by mail from specialists in cacti and other succulents; see Chapter 11 for addresses.

Gasteria

PRONUNCIATION: gas-TEER-ee-uh

COMMON NAME: Gasteria.

USES: Desktop, sill, or open terrarium.

LEAF COLOR: Dark or light green, sometimes with white variegation.

FLOWERS: Green, salmon, scarlet.

Environmental Needs

LIGHT: Sunny east, south, or west window; adapts to fluorescent-light garden.

TEMPERATURE: 62–75°F.

HUMIDITY: Low.

MIST FREQUENTLY: No.

SOIL MIX: Cactus or all-purpose.

SOIL MOISTURE: Evenly moist to nearly dry.

PROPAGATION: By division.

PROBLEMS: Constantly wet, poorly drained soil may cause the roots to rot.

COMMENTS: These succulent plants are able to withstand underwatering. The foliage is always attractive; sculptural in quality, and when the flowers appears they are always graceful and subtly colored.

Gibasis

PRONUNCIATION: jib-BAY-sis

COMMON NAME: Tahitian bridal veil.

USES: Hanging basket or pedestal.

LEAF COLOR: Olive-green with purplish undersides.

FLOWERS: White.

Environmental Needs

LIGHT: Sunny east or west window, or a few feet back from a sunny south window; tolerates bright north, or similar light with little or no direct sun.

TEMPERATURE: 62–75°F.

HUMIDITY: Medium; tolerates less.

MIST FREQUENTLY: Yes, if convenient.

Fittonia, the nerve plant, may have either white or rosy pink veins, depending on the variety.

The variegated leaves of furcraea, a succulent.

SOIL MIX: All-purpose.
SOIL MOISTURE: Evenly moist to on the dry side.
PROPAGATION: Tip cuttings.
PROBLEMS: If the soil dries out severely, older leaves will die, and tips on younger ones may turn brown.
COMMENTS: This plant needs to be pinched back frequently in order to encourage compact, full growth.

Ginger: See **Zingiber**

Grapefruit: See **Citrus**

Grape-ivy: See **Cissus**

Gymnocalycium

PRONUNCIATION: jim-noh-kal-ISS-ee-um
COMMON NAME: Chin cactus, rose plaid cactus, red cap, Oriental moon.
USES: Desktop, sill, or open terrarium.
LEAF COLOR: Green, gray, brown, blue-green, red, yellow.
FLOWERS: Pink, white.

Environmental Needs
LIGHT: Sunny east, south, or west window; adapts well to a fluorescent-light garden.
TEMPERATURE: 55–70°F during the winter heating season.
HUMIDITY: Low.
MIST FREQUENTLY: No.
SOIL MIX: Cactus.
SOIL MOISTURE: Evenly moist to nearly dry; be careful to keep mostly on the dry side during the winter.
PROPAGATION: By removing offsets if they form.
PROBLEMS: Wet, poorly drained soil, especially in the winter, may cause the roots to rot.

Gymnocalycium
quehlianum,
a chin-cactus.

Author

COMMENTS: These fascinating, colorful, small cacti
are available in many species and varieties and make
interesting collector plants; unusual kinds are available by mail from specialists (see Chapter 11 for
addresses).

Haworthia

PRONUNCIATION: ha-WORTH-ee-uh
COMMON NAME: Haworthia.
USES: Desktop, sill, or open terrarium.
LEAF COLOR: Various shades of green.
FLOWERS: Rarely in cultivation.

Environmental Needs
LIGHT: Sunny east, south, or west window; grows well
in a fluorescent-light garden.
TEMPERATURE: 62–75°F.

HUMIDITY: Low.
MIST FREQUENTLY: No.
SOIL MIX: Cactus or all-purpose.
SOIL MOISTURE: Evenly moist to on the dry side.
PROPAGATION: By division or removal of offsets.
PROBLEMS: Wet, poorly drained soil may cause the roots to rot.
COMMENTS: These succulent plants are easily cultivated and tolerant of underwatering.

Hearts entangled: See **Ceropegia**

Hedera

PRONUNCIATION: HED-er-uh
COMMON NAME: English ivy.
USES: Desktop, sill, hanging basket, pedestal, or terrarium.
LEAF COLOR: Green, gray-green, white, gold.
FLOWERS: No.

Environmental Needs
LIGHT: Bright light or near a sunny east, south, or west window; does well in a fluorescent-light garden.
TEMPERATURE: 55–70°F. during the winter heating season.
HUMIDITY: Medium; tolerates less if the soil is evenly moist and the temperature is not above 72°F.
MIST FREQUENTLY: Yes.
SOIL MIX: African violet or all-purpose.
SOIL MOISTURE: Evenly moist.
PROPAGATION: Tip cuttings.
PROBLEMS: Red spider-mite is likely to attack hedera in air that is hot, dry, and stale. If the soil dries out severely, many leaves will die and possibly entire branches.

There are many varieties of hedra (English ivy). This one has miniature leaves and would be an excellent choice for a terrarium landscape.

COMMENTS: English ivy makes an excellent plant for a weekend house kept at around 50–55°F during weekdays in the winter; just be sure the soil is well-moistened before you go away.

Helxine

PRONUNCIATION: hel-ZYE-nee
COMMON NAME: Baby's tears.
USES: Desktop, sill, hanging basket, pedestal, or terrarium.
LEAF COLOR: Green or golden green.
FLOWERS: No.

Environmental Needs
LIGHT: Bright light or a few feet back from a sunny window; thrives in a fluorescent-light garden.
TEMPERATURE: 62–72°F.
HUMIDITY: Medium; tolerates less.
MIST FREQUENTLY: Yes, if convenient.
SOIL MIX: African violet or terrarium.
SOIL MOISTURE: Evenly moist to wet.
PROPAGATION: By division or tip cuttings.
PROBLEMS: Excessive heat and dry soil in combination will quickly wither the delicate leaves and stems of baby's-tears.

Holly fern: See Cyrtomium

Howeia

PRONUNCIATION: HOW-ee-uh
COMMON NAME: Kent palm.
USES: Floor shrub or tree effect.
LEAF COLOR: Green.
FLOWERS: No.

Helxine or baby's-tears is seen here as a hanging-basket plant.

Environmental Needs

LIGHT: Near a sunny east, south, or west window; does fairly well in a bright exposure but without sun shining directly on the fronds.

TEMPERATURE: 62–72°F.

HUMIDITY: Medium; tolerates less.

MIST FREQUENTLY: Yes, if convenient.

SOIL MIX: All-purpose.

SOIL MOISTURE: Evenly moist.

PROPAGATION: By division, but difficult.

PROBLEMS: In hot, dry, stale air, red spider-mite may attack. If the soil dries out severely, leaf tips will die.

COMMENTS: This is one of the best of the large palms to cultivate indoors; it is coarser in appearance than the common areca, but *far* superior and worth the considerable price you will have to pay for a sizable, healthy specimen.

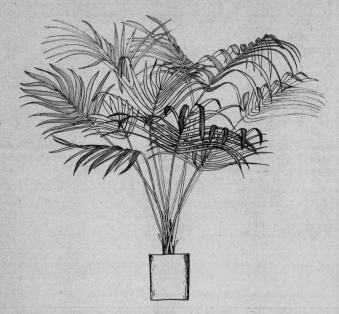

Howeia, the kentia palm, is perhaps best of all large palms to grow as a permanent house plant.

Hoya

PRONUNCIATION: HOY-uh
COMMON NAME: Waxplant.
USES: Desktop, sill, hanging basket, pedestal, or terrarium.
LEAF COLOR: Green, silver, white, rose-pink.
FLOWERS: White and pink; fragrant.

Environmental Needs
LIGHT: Sunny east, south, or west window; adapts to bright light with little or no sun shining directly on the leaves; thrives in a fluorescent-light garden.

TEMPERATURE: 62–75°F.
HUMIDITY: Medium; tolerates less.
MIST FREQUENTLY: Yes, if convenient.
SOIL MIX: All-purpose.
SOIL MOISTURE: Evenly moist to on the dry side.
PROPAGATION: Tip cuttings.
PROBLEMS: Hoya is virtually trouble-free.
COMMENTS: Tip cuttings of hoya placed in a glass or
    vase of water will root and grow there for months;
    maintain the water level and once a month pour out
    all the old and replace with fresh.

Impatiens

PRONUNCIATION: im-PAY-shenz
COMMON NAME: Sultana.
USES: Desktop, sill hanging basket, pedestal.
LEAF COLOR: Green, sometimes variegated with
    cream, gold, pink, or orange.
FLOWERS: White, pink, red, salmon, orange, lavender,
    cerise.

Environmental Needs
LIGHT: Sunny east, south, or west window in winter;
    less direct sun is needed in the summer indoors.
    Thrives in a fluorescent-light garden.
TEMPERATURE: 62–72°F during the winter heating
    season.
HUMIDITY: Medium.
MIST FREQUENTLY: Yes, if convenient.
SOIL MIX: All-purpose.
SOIL MOISTURE: Evenly moist.
PROPAGATION: Seeds or tip cuttings.
PROBLEMS: Red spider-mite is likely to attack if the
    air is hot, dry, and stale. If the soil dries out severely,
    causing the leaves to wilt, much of the foliage will die
    as well as any developing flower buds.

Cyclone impatiens, here surrounded by the foliage of aspara-gus-fern, has colorful leaves as well as beautiful flowers.

Variegated kalanchoe of this type makes an excellent house plant in a sunny window.

COMMENTS: Cyclone hybirds recently developed from species discovered in New Guinea have showy foliage and unusually large flowers.

Indian laurel: See **Ficus**

Ivy, English: See **Hedera**

Jade plant: See **Crassula**

Kaffir lily: See **Clivia**

Kalanchoe

PRONUNCIATION: kal-an-KOH-ee
COMMON NAME: Kalanchoe.
USES: Desktop, sill, floor shrub (specimen-sized *K. beharensis*), hanging basket or pedestal (*K. uniflora*).
LEAF COLOR: Green, blue-green, or brownish.
FLOWERS: Scarlet, orange, apricot, yellow.

Environmental Needs
LIGHT: Sunny east, south, or west window.
TEMPERATURE: 62–75°F.
HUMIDITY: Low.
MIST FREQUENTLY: No.
SOIL MIX: All-purpose.
SOIL MOISTURE: Evenly moist to on the dry side.
PROPAGATION: Tip or leaf cuttings, or seeds.
PROBLEMS: Mealybugs sometimes attack kalanchoes. Insufficient sunlight causes undersized, malformed leaves. The flower-covered *K. blossfeldiana* varieties sold by florists are difficult to keep as permanent plants.

Kangaroo vine: See **Cissus**

Kentia palm: See **Howeia**

Laurus

PRONUNCIATION: LAW-russ
COMMON NAME: Sweet bay.
USES: Desktop or sill.
LEAF COLOR: Green.
FLOWERS: No.

Environmental Needs
LIGHT: Sunny east, south, or west window.
TEMPERATURE: 55–70°F during the winter heating season.
HUMIDITY: Medium.
MIST FREQUENTLY: Yes, if convenient.
SOIL MIX: All-purpose or African violet.
SOIL MOISTURE: Evenly moist.
PROPAGATION: Tip cuttings, but difficult.
PROBLEMS: Excessive heat and dry soil in combination may kill sweet bay, but if the soil is kept evenly moist it will tolerate warmer temperatures.
COMMENTS: This is the sweet bay which provides the leaves used for seasoning. Plants are available by mail from herb specialists; see Chapter 11 for addresses.

Lemaireocereus

PRONUNCIATION: le-mare-ee-oh-SEER-ee-us
COMMON NAME: Organ-pipe cactus.
USES: Floor shrub, tree effect, or as living sculpture on a pedestal.
LEAF GREEN: Green.
FLOWERS: White, yellow, red, greenish.

Environmental Needs
LIGHT: Sunny east, south, or west window.

Kalanchoe blossfeldiana *varieties like this one are usually given or received as florist gift plants. They are difficult to keep over and re-flower.*

TEMPERATURE: 62–72°F.
HUMIDITY: Low.
MIST FREQUENTLY: No.
SOIL MIX: Cactus or all-purpose.
SOIL MOISTURE: Evenly moist to on the dry side.
PROPAGATION: Removal of offsets.
PROBLEMS: Wet, poorly drained soil, especially in the
winter, is likely to cause the roots to rot.
COMMENTS: When you buy a specimen columnar
cactus, be sure it has been nursery-grown and not
recently transplanted from the desert.

Lemon: See **Citrus**

Lily-of-the-Nile: See **Agapanthus**

Lily-turf: See **Ophiopogon**

Lime: See **Citrus**

Lipstick vine: See **Aeschynanthus**

Lobivia

PRONUNCIATION: loh-BIV-ee-uh
COMMON NAME: Lobivia, a cactus.
USES: Desktop, sill, or open terrarium.
LEAF COLOR: Green.
FLOWERS: Red, yellow.

Environmental Needs
LIGHT: Sunny east, south, or west window.
TEMPERATURE: 62–72°F during the winter heating
season.
HUMIDITY: Low.
MIST FREQUENTLY: No.
SOIL MIX: Cactus or all-purpose.
SOIL MOISTURE: Evenly moist to on the dry side.

Maranta or prayer plant is easy to grow, but letting the soil dry out severely causes the leaf tips to turn yellow and brown.

PROPAGATION: By removing offsets.

PROBLEMS: Wet, poorly drained soil, especially in the winter, is likely to cause the roots to rot.

COMMENTS: One of the best small, flowering cactus to grow as a house plant.

Madagascar dragon tree: See **Dracaena**

Mammillaria

PRONUNCIATION: mam-mil-LAY-ree-uh
COMMON NAME: Mammillaria, a cactus.
USES: Desktop, sill, on a pedestal as living sculpture, or in an open terrarium.
LEAF COLOR: Green, but often nearly covered with white hairs and variously colored spines.
FLOWERS: Pink, red, white, yellow.

Environmental Needs
LIGHT: Sunny east, south, or west window.
TEMPERATURE: 50–60°F in winter to induce bloom.
HUMIDITY: Low.
MIST FREQUENTLY: No.
SOIL MIX: Cactus or all-purpose.
SOIL MOISTURE: Evenly moist to nearly dry in spring and summer; nearly dry in fall and winter.
PROPAGATION: By removing offsets.
PROBLEMS: Too much warmth and moisture in winter will prevent flowering.
COMMENTS: A large and varied group of cacti, great fun to collect; unusual kinds are available by mail from specialists (see Chapter 11 for addresses).

Maranta

PRONUNCIATION: muh-RANT-uh
COMMON NAME: Prayer plant.
USES: Desktop, sill, hanging basket, pedestal, or in a fairly large terrarium.
LEAF COLOR: Green with reddish brown or pink markings.
FLOWERS: White, but insignificant.

Environmental Needs

LIGHT: Bright light but little or no direct sun.

TEMPERATURE: 62–75°F.

HUMIDITY: Medium.

MIST FREQUENTLY: Yes, but not absolutely necessary.

SOIL MIX: African violet or terrarium.

SOIL MOISTURE: Evenly moist.

PROPAGATION: By division.

PROBLEMS: Severely dry soil causes older leaves to shrivel up and die and the tips of younger ones to turn brown.

COMMENTS: Use scissors to clip off the stems of dead leaves; if you try to pull them, you may break or uproot the entire plant.

Author

When this neoregelia, a bromeliad, is about ready to flower, the normally green leaves in the center of the plant turn to glowing yellow and orange.

Medicine plant: See **Aloe**

Milkbush: See **Euphorbia**

Minature sweet flag: See **Acorus**

Mother-in-law's tongue: See **Sansevieria**

Neoregelia

PRONUNCIATION: nee-oh-ruh-JEE-lee-uh
COMMON NAME: Bromeliad.
USES: Desktop, sill, or pedestal.
LEAF COLOR: Green, white, cream, brilliant rose-pink.
FLOWERS: White, blue, lilac, red.

Environmental Needs
LIGHT: Sunny east, south, or west window; tolerates bright light without direct sun indefinitely if mature to begin with; thrives in a fluorescent-light garden.
TEMPERATURE: 62–75°F.
HUMIDITY: Medium; tolerates less.
MIST FREQUENTLY: Yes.
SOIL MIX: Cactus.
SOIL MOISTURE: Evenly moist to nearly dry; once a week, fill cup formed by leaves with clean water, but pour out old water before adding fresh.
PROPAGATION: By division, usually a few months after the plant has flowered.
PROBLEMS: None, unless roots stand in water for long periods of time, in which case the roots may rot.
COMMENTS: Several different neoregelias are available from specialists (see Chapter 11 for addresses).

Nephrolepis

PRONUNCIATION: neff-roh-LEEP-iss

COMMON NAME: Boston fern; fluffy ruffles.
USES: Desktop, sill, hanging basket, pedestal.
LEAF COLOR: Green.
FLOWERS: No.

Environmental Needs
LIGHT: Bright light; some direct sun is acceptable during the winter months. Thrives in a fluorescent-light garden, but may become too large.
TEMPERATURE: 62–72°F during the winter heating season.
HUMIDITY: Medium.
MIST FREQUENTLY: Yes.
SOIL MIX: African violet or terrarium.
SOIL MOISTURE: Evenly moist.
PROPAGATION: By division.
PROBLEMS: Severely dry soil, or drafts of hot, dry air cause fronds to die; wet, poorly drained soil may cause the roots to rot.
COMMENTS: Boston fern and its varieties such as fluffy ruffles have the puzzling habit of growing like weeds for some people and being temperamental for others.

Nephthytis: See **Syngonium**

Nerve plant: See **Fittonia**

Night jessamine: See **Cestrum**

Norfolk Island pine: See **Araucaria**

Ocimum

PRONUNCIATION: OH-sim-um
COMMON NAME: Basil.
USES: Sill.

'Fluffy Ruffles' is a form of Boston fern, a nephrolepis.

LEAF COLOR: Green or purple.
FLOWERS: White, but insignificant.

Environmental Needs
LIGHT: Sunny east, south, or west window; thrives in
   a fluorescent-light garden.

TEMPERATURE: 62–75°F.
HUMIDITY: Medium.
MIST FREQUENTLY: Yes, if convenient.
SOIL MIX: All-purpose.
SOIL MOISTURE: Evenly moist.
PROPAGATION: Grow from seeds.
PROBLEMS: Mealybugs may attack basil.
COMMENTS: Frequent pinching back helps encourage compact, full growth; use the pinchings for seasoning. Discard old plants and start over with seedlings every six months.

Ophiopogon

PRONUNCIATION: oh-fee-oh-POH-gon
COMMON NAME: Lily-turf.
USES: Desktop, sill, hanging basket, or pedestal.
LEAF COLOR: Green and white.
FLOWERS: White or lavender, but rarely in the house.

Environmental Needs

LIGHT: Near a sunny east, south, or west window, but avoid long periods of hot sun shining directly on the leaves; thrives in a fluorescent-light garden.
TEMPERATURE: 62–72°F during the winter heating season.
MIST FREQUENTLY: Yes, if convenient.
HUMIDITY: Medium, but tolerates less.
SOIL MIX: All-purpose.
SOIL MOISTURE: Evenly moist.
PROPAGATION: By division.
PROBLEMS: Severely dry soil causes the leaf tips to die. Red spider-mites may attack in air that is hot, dry, and stale.
COMMENTS: This is an excellent foliage house plant

Author

Not all opuntias are miniature cacti like this one, but many of them make excellent house plants in a sunny window.

which you are likely to find only among nursery stock of outdoor perennials and ground covers.

Opuntia

PRONUNCIATION: oh-PUNT-ee-uh
COMMON NAME: Prickly pear cactus.
USES: Desktop, sill, floor shrub, as living sculpture on a pedestal; small kinds may be planted in an open terrarium.
LEAF COLOR: Green or blue-green.
FLOWERS: Rarely indoors.

Environmental Needs
LIGHT: Sunny east, south, or west window.
TEMPERATURE: 60–75°F during the winter heating season.
HUMIDITY: Low.
MIST FREQUENTLY: No.
SOIL MIX: Cactus or all-purpose.
SOIL MOISTURE: Evenly moist to on the dry side in spring and summer; mostly on the dry side in fall and winter.
PROPAGATION: Cuttings of the pads.
PROBLEMS: Insufficient light causes spindly, under-sized new growth. Wet, poorly drained soil is likely to cause the roots to rot.
COMMENTS: There are many different kinds and sizes of opuntia available by mail from specialists; see Chapter 11 for addresses.

Orange: See **Citrus**

Oriental moon cactus: See **Gymnocalycium**

Oxalis

PRONUNCIATION: OX-uh-liss

Oxalis regnellii *provides a constant display of white flowers.*

COMMON NAME: Oxalis.
USES: Desktop, sill, hanging basket, pedestal.
LEAF COLOR: Green or green and yellow.
FLOWERS: White, pink.

Environmental Needs
LIGHT: Sunny east, south, or west window; thrives in a fluorescent-light garden.
TEMPERATURE: 62–75°F.
HUMIDITY: Medium.
MIST FREQUENTLY: Yes, if convenient.
SOIL MIX: All-purpose.
SOIL MOISTURE: Evenly moist.
PROPAGATION: By division.
PROBLEMS: Red spider-mites may attack if air is hot, dry, and stale; watch for mealybugs.
COMMENTS: There are many kinds of oxalis in cultivation, but the three most easily cultivated as all-year house plants are *O. rubra* (sometimes listed as *O. crassipes;* green leaves, rose-pink flowers), *O. regnellii* (olive-green leaves, white flowers), and *O. martiana aureo-reticulata* (green leaves veined with yellow and pink flowers). These are seldom seen in local plant shops, but they are available by mail from such specialists as Logees and Merry Gardens; see Chapter 11 for addresses.

Palm: See **Caryota, Chamaedorea, Chamaerops, Chrysalidocarpus, Howeia**

Panama hat plant: See **Carludovica**

Pandanus

PRONUNCIATION: pan-DAY-nus
COMMON NAME: Screw-pine.
USES: Floor shrub, hanging basket, or pedestal.

LEAF COLOR: Green and white.
FLOWERS: No.

Environmental Needs

LIGHT: Near a sunny east, south, or west window; tolerates long periods in bright light with little or no direct sun.
TEMPERATURE: 62–75°F.
HUMIDITY: Medium; tolerates less.
MIST FREQUENTLY: Yes, if convenient.
SOIL MIX: All-purpose.
SOIL MOISTURE: Evenly moist to on the dry side.
PROPAGATION: By removing offsets.
PROBLEMS: In hot, dry, stale air, red spider-mites may attack. Severely dry soil may cause leaf tips to die.
COMMENTS: A well-grown, symmetrical screw-pine

Maddy Miller

Pandanus or screw-pine forms graceful, symmetrical rosettes of green-and-white leaves.

makes a stunning plant to display on a pedestal, but there are sharp spines along the leaf edges, so be sure to position it where no one is likely to brush against the plant.

Peace lily: See **Spathiphyllum**

Pencil plant: See **Euphorbia**

Peperomia

PRONUNCIATION: pep-er-OH-mee-uh
COMMON NAME: Peperomia; watermelon begonia.
USES: Desktop, still, hanging basket, pedestal, terrarium.
LEAF COLOR: Green, silver, white.
FLOWERS: Yes, but insignificant.

Environmental Needs
LIGHT: Near a sunny east, south, or west window, but full sun shining directly on the leaves for long periods of time is not desirable. Thrives in a fluorescent-light garden.
TEMPERATURE: 62–75°F.
HUMIDITY: Low to medium.
MIST FREQUENTLY: No.
SOIL MIX: All-purpose.
SOIL MOISTURE: Evenly moist to on the dry side.
PROPAGATION: By division or leaf cuttings.
PROBLEMS: Severely dry soil, to the point of wilting the leaves, will cause many of them to collapse and die, the same as will wet, poorly drained soil.
COMMENTS: Common peperomias are available from most local plant shops; more unusual ones are listed by mail-order specialists, especially Alberts & Merkel (see Chapter 11 for address).

Peperomia leaves may be green, silver or white, sometimes with reddish-brown veins and stems.

Persea

PRONUNCIATION: PURSE-ee-uh
COMMON NAME: Avocado.
USES: Floor shrub or tree.
LEAF COLOR: Green.
FLOWERS: No.

Environmental Needs

LIGHT: Sunny east, south, or west window; adapts to bright light with little or no direct sun shining on the leaves.

TEMPERATURE: 62–72°F.

HUMIDITY: Medium; tolerates less.

MIST FREQUENTLY: Yes, if convenient.

SOIL MIX: All-purpose.

SOIL MOISTURE: Evenly moist.

PROPAGATION: Snuggle the larger, fatter part of the avocado pit in a pot of moist soil, leaving the top half exposed. When the sprout is 12 inches tall, cut it back to six inches. This drastic pruning is vital to the future bushiness and health of the avocado.

PROBLEMS: If the soil in which an avocado is growing dries out severely, many of the older leaves will die, and brown edges and spots will develop in the others. Drafts of hot, dry air are also not to the liking of avocado.

Philodendron

PRONUNCIATION: phil-oh-DEN-dron

COMMON NAME: Philodendron.

USES: Desktop, sill, floor shrub, hanging basket, pedestal (possibly for tree effect, depending on the size and kind of philodendron); small-growing silverleaf *P. soidiroi* grows well in a terrarium.

LEAF COLOR: Green, burgundy, yellow, white, silver.

FLOWERS: No.

Environmental Needs

LIGHT: Near a sunny east, south, or west window, but long periods of hot sun shining directly on the leaves

Bill Mulligan

Pits of persea, known otherwise as avocado, are seen here rooting in glasses of water; the one on the left grew its sprout to 12 inches tall and has now been cut back to induce healthier, better shaped future growth.

are not required. Adapts to bright light with little or
no direct sun.

TEMPERATURE: 62–75°F.

HUMIDITY: Medium; tolerates less.

MIST FREQUENTLY: Yes, if convenient.

SOIL MIX: African violet, terrarium, or all-purpose.

SOIL MOISTURE: Evenly moist.

PROPAGATION: Tip cuttings.

PROBLEMS: Severely dry soil causes older leaves to
turn yellow and die. Mealybugs sometimes attack
philodendrons. Constantly wet, poorly drained soil

228

may cause the roots to rot; philodendrons are also sensitive to overfeeding.

COMMENTS: Philodendrons which require a moist totem pole on which to climb do not generally make very good house plants; see section on "Other Problems" in Chapter 9. Better philodendrons to grow as

California Avocado Advisory Board

Within a year's time, a persea or avocado seedling may be several feet tall as this one is.

house plants include the self-heading or bush-forming types such as *P. selloum* and the small-leaved creepers or climbers such as *P. oxycardium* and *P. sodiroi*. More unusual kinds that make excellent house plants are available by mail from Alberts & Merkel (see Chapter 11 for address).

Piggyback (pickaback) plant: See **Tolmiea**

Pilea

PRONUNCIATION: pie-LEE-uh
COMMON NAME: Aluminum plant (*P. cadierei*), artillery fern (*P. microphylla*), creeping Charlie (*P. nummulariifolia*).
USES: Desktop, sill, hanging basket, pedestal, terrarium.
LEAF COLOR: Green, silver, bronze.
FLOWERS: Yes, but insignificant.

Environmental Needs
LIGHT: Bright light, little direct sun needed; thrives in a fluorescent-light garden.
TEMPERATURE: 62–75°F.
HUMIDITY: Medium; tolerates less.
MIST FREQUENTLY: Yes, if convenient.
SOIL MIX: All-purpose.
SOIL MOISTURE: Evenly moist.
PROPAGATION: By tip cuttings.
PROBLEMS: Severely dry soil causes old leaves to die and tips of those remaining to turn brown. Pinch back frequently to encourage full, compact growth.
COMMENTS: Specialists list other pileas, including the variety "Moon Valley" which has pebbly surfaced leaves of green, chartreuse, and reddish brown; for addresses, see Chapter 11.

230

Maddy Miller

'Red Duchess' philodenron has dark green leaves set on red stems.

Pineapple: See **Ananas**

Platycerium

> PRONUNCIATION: platt-iss-SEER-ee-um
> COMMON NAME: Staghorn fern.
> USES: If young and small, may be cultivated in a terrarium; grow larger specimens in a hanging basket, or hung on a wall.
> LEAF COLOR: Green.
> FLOWERS: No.

Environmental Needs
LIGHT: Bright light but little or no sun shining directly

231

on the leaves; young plants thrive in a fluorescent-light garden.

TEMPERATURE: 62–75°F.

HUMIDITY: Medium.

MIST FREQUENTLY: Yes.

SOIL MIX: Osmunda fern fiber (available from orchid specialists) and unmilled sphagnum moss.

SOIL MOISTURE: Evenly moist.

PROPAGATION: By removing offsets.

PROBLEMS: Avoid hanging where drafts of hot, dry air will blow directly on a staghorn, otherwise the fronds may die back. Once a week, soak piece of bark or osmunda on which the fern is mounted in tepid water for a few minutes; remove, drain, then hang back up.

COMMENTS: The bizarre staghorn fern is not the easiest house plant to grow, but on the other hand, it is not impossibly difficult.

Plectranthus

PRONUNCIATION: pleck-TRANTH-us

COMMON NAME: Swedish ivy.

USES: Hanging basket or pedestal.

LEAF COLOR: Green or green and white.

FLOWERS: No.

Environmental Needs

LIGHT: In or near a sunny east, south, or west window; adapts to less light, but leaves and stems may be spindly; young plants thrive in a fluorescent-light garden.

TEMPERATURE: 62–75°F.

HUMIDITY: Medium; tolerates less.

MIST FREQUENTLY: Yes, if convenient.

SOIL MIX: All-purpose.

Author

'Moon Valley' pilea is a small and easy-to-grow house plant for the beginner.

Author

Pilea microphylla *is the old-fashioned artillery-fern, another easy plant for the beginner.*

233

Staghorn fern (platycerium) makes a bizarre appearance and deserves special treatment all around, from routine care to dramatic lighting at night.

Author

HUMIDITY: Medium; tolerates less.

MIST FREQUENTLY: Yes, if convenient.

SOIL MIX: All-purpose.

SOIL MOISTURE: Evenly moist.

PROPAGATION: Tip cuttings.

PROBLEMS: Relatively trouble-free. Severely dry soil causes all of the older leaves to wither and die quickly.

COMMENTS: Swedish ivy is one of the best all-around house plants. If the soil is never allowed to dry out, it is surprisingly tolerant of drafts of hot air, for example, when it is hung in a window over a heating unit. To encourage full, compact growth, pinch back frequently. When stems near the base become woody and leafless, it is time to start new plants from tip cuttings.

Pleomele

PRONUNCIATION: plee-OH-may-lee
COMMON NAME: Pleomele.
USES: Desktop, sill, floor shrub, tree effect, or pedestal.
LEAF COLOR: Green.
FLOWERS: White, but rare as a house plant.

Environmental Needs
LIGHT: Bright light but not more than an hour or two of sun shining directly on the leaves.
TEMPERATURE: 62–75°F.
HUMIDITY: Medium; tolerates less.
MIST FREQUENTLY: Yes, if convenient.
SOIL MIX: All-purpose.
SOIL MOISTURE: Evenly moist to wet.
PROPAGATION: Tip cuttings.
PROBLEMS: Severely dry soil causes the leaf tips to turn brown and die. A remarkably trouble-free plant.
COMMENTS: Specimen pleomeles as much as eight feet tall and four feet across are occasionally available; one of these, when dramatically lighted at night, makes a beautiful living sculpture.

Plover eggs: See **Adromischus**

Podocarpus

PRONUNCIATION: poh-doh-KARP-us
COMMON NAME: Podocarpus.
USES: Floor shrub or tree effect.
LEAF COLOR: Green.
FLOWERS: No.

LIGHT: In or near a sunny east, south, or west window. Good keeper for several months in low light.
TEMPERATURE: 60–70°F during the winter heating season.
HUMIDITY: Medium.

Maddy Miller

Plectranthus australis, *the Swedish-ivy, is nearly an ideal hanging-basket plant, but for best results, pinch out the growing tips frequently to encourage compact, full growth.*

MIST FREQUENTLY: Yes, if convenient.
SOIL MIX: All-purpose.
SOIL MOISTURE: Evenly moist.
PROPAGATION: Tip cuttings, but fairly difficult.
PROBLEMS: Severely dry soil will cause the leaf tips to turn brown. Avoid placing where drafts of hot, dry air blow directly on the leaves.
COMMENTS: A durable, pest-free, large foliage plant.

Polypodium

PRONUNCIATION: polly-POH-dee-um
COMMON NAME: *P. aureum* is the bear's-paw or hare's foot fern.
USES: Hanging basket or pedestal.
LEAF COLOR: Green or blue-green.
FLOWERS: No.

Environmental Needs
LIGHT: Bright light but little or no direct sun.
TEMPERATURE: 62–75°F.
HUMIDITY: Medium.
MIST FREQUENTLY: Yes, if convenient.
SOIL MIX: African violet or terrarium.
SOIL MOISTURE: Evenly moist.
PROPAGATION: By cuttings of the rhizome.
PROBLEMS: A durable, pest-free fern. Severely dry soil, or soggy wet, poorly drained soil may cause this fern to die.
COMMENTS: The polypodium grows large and makes a bold appearance, especially when displayed on a pedestal and down- or uplighted at night.

Polyscias

PRONUNCIATION: poh-liss-EE-us
COMMON NAME: Aralia.

A specimen polypodium or bear's-paw fern makes a memorable sight when displayed on a pedestal as this one is and given a floodlight at night.

USES: Desktop, sill, floor shrub, tree effect, pedestal.
LEAF COLOR: Green or green and white.
FLOWERS: No.

Environmental Needs
LIGHT: Near a bright or sunny window, but sun shin-
ing directly on the leaves for more than an hour or
two is not required.
TEMPERATURE: 62–75°F.
HUMIDITY: Medium; tolerates less.
MIST FREQUENTLY: Yes, if convenient.
SOIL MIX: All-purpose.
SOIL MOISTURE: Evenly moist.
PROPAGATION: Cuttings of partly mature stems.
PROBLEMS: Polyscias resents being moved around,
even within the same room. When you bring one
home, it is almost certain to lose a quantity of the
older leaves, but if you give it thoughtful care, healthy
growth should resume. Do not begin applying fertilizer until the plant has obviously made a satisfactory adjustment. Either soggy wet, poorly drained
soil or severely dry soil will cause polyscias to shed
leaves.

Ponytail: See **Beaucarnea**

Portulacaria

PRONUNCIATION: port-yew-luh-KAY-ree-uh
COMMON NAME: Elephant bush.
USES: Desktop, sill, floor shrub, or open terrarium.
LEAF COLOR: Green or gray-green, white and pink.
FLOWERS: No.

Environmental Needs
LIGHT: Sunny east, south, or west window.
TEMPERATURE: 62–72°F.

Polyscias balfouri- ana marginata *has rounded green leaves edged with white. It grows to indoor-tree size.*

Author

HUMIDITY: Low.
MIST FREQUENTLY: No.
SOIL MIX: All-purpose.
SOIL MOISTURE: Evenly moist to on the dry side.
PROPAGATION: Tip cuttings.
PROBLEMS: Trouble-free unless overwatered, in which case the roots may rot.

Pothos: See **Scindapsus**

Prayer plant: See **Maranta**

Queen's-tears: See **Billbergia**

Rabbit's-foot fern: See **Davallia**

Red cap cactus: See **Gymnocalycium**

Rosary vine: See **Ceropegia**

Sago palm: See **Cycas**

Saintpaulia

>   PRONUNCIATION: saint-PAUL-ee-uh
>   COMMON NAME: African violet.
>   USES: Desktop, sill, hanging basket, pedestal, terrarium.
>   LEAF COLOR: Green or green and white.
>   FLOWERS: White, blue, lavender, purple, pink, wine-red.

Author

Polyscias fruticosa has lacy leaves, light green when young, but turning darker with age. It grows to indoor-tree size.

Environmental Needs

LIGHT: Bright light or near a sunny east, south, or west window; thrives in a fluorescent-light garden.

TEMPERATURE: 62–75°F.

HUMIDITY: Medium.

MIST FREQUENTLY: No.

SOIL MIX: African violet.

SOIL MOISTURE: Evenly moist.

PROPAGATION: By division or leaf cuttings.

PROBLEMS: Mealybugs and cyclamen mite favor African violets. Watering the roots with cold water, or splashing the leaves with it, causes yellow spots to form. Severely dry soil causes older leaves to wilt and die, as well as developing flower buds. Too much

George W. Park Seed Co., Inc.

Many newer varieties of African violet (saintpaulia) have double, frilled or star-shaped flowers—and sometimes all three traits in one, as shown here.

242

hot sun shining directly on the leaves will burn spots in them; lack of light results in pale leaves on long spindly stems and prevents flowering.

COMMENTS: Hybrid African violets available by mail from specialists come in hundreds of different varieties; see Chapter 11 for addresses.

Sansevieria

PRONUNCIATION: san-zuh-VEER-ee-uh

COMMON NAME: Snake plant, mother-in-law's tongue.

USES: Desktop, sill, pedestal.

LEAF COLOR: Green, silver, gold.

FLOWERS: White and fragrant, but rarely.

Environmental Needs

LIGHT: Thrives in a range between low light and a sunny south window; grows well in artificial light.

Author

With a reflector containing two 20-watt fluorescent tubes you can grow a small collection like this one which occupies one shelf of a storage unit and room divider.

Sansevierias come in a variety of sizes and shapes; all are among the easiest of all house plants to grow.

TEMPERATURE: 62–75°F.

HUMIDITY: Low.

MIST FREQUENTLY: No.

SOIL MIX: All-purpose.

SOIL MOISTURE: By division.

PROBLEMS: None.

COMMENTS: Sansevierias are absolutely fail-safe house plants. Specialists offer unusual kinds seldom seen in local shops; see Chapter 11 for addresses.

Schlumbergera

PRONUNCIATION: schum-BERJ-er-uh

COMMON NAME: Christmas cactus.

USES: Desktop, sill, hanging basket, pedestal.

LEAF COLOR: Green.

FLOWERS: White, pink, salmon, red.

Environmental Needs

LIGHT: Bright light or in a sunny east or west window, or near a sunny south window.

TEMPERATURE: 60–72°F.

HUMIDITY: Medium; tolerates less.

MIST FREQUENTLY: Yes, if convenient.

SOIL MIX: All-purpose or cactus.

SOIL MOISTURE: Evenly moist to on the dry side.

PROPAGATION: Tip cuttings.

PROBLEMS: Failure to bloom is the main complaint about Christmas cactus. To encourage bloom, keep in a cool place in autumn (September–November) and water only enough to keep the soil from drying out severely; do not apply fertilizer during this time, and be sure that artificial light does not shine on the plant during the normal hours of darkness in autumn. Around Thanksgiving resume normal care; flowering should occur.

Scilla

PRONUNCIATION: SILL-uh

COMMON NAME: *S. violacea* is sometimes called silver squill.

USES: Desktop, sill, hanging basket, or terrarium.

LEAF COLOR: Olive-green, silver, burgundy.

FLOWERS: White to pale lavender, but relatively insignificant.

Environmental Needs

LIGHT: In or near a sunny east, south, or west window; thrives in a fluorescent-light garden.

TEMPERATURE: 62–72°F.

HUMIDITY: Medium, tolerates less.

MIST FREQUENTLY: No.

SOIL MIX: All-purpose.

Christmas cactus or schlumbergera is an excellent plant to display on a pedestal so that the graceful stems can cascade freely.

Scilla violacea *is an unusual small house plant with exquisite foliage; it is also easy to grow.*

SOIL MOISTURE: Evenly moist.
PROPAGATION: By division.
PROBLEMS: Mostly trouble-free. Severely dry soil will cause older leaves to turn yellow and die, but this plant grows from a succulent bulb and can survive considerable neglect and lack of water.
COMMENTS: A beautiful, small foliage house plant that is very easy to grow. If you can't find it locally, order it from a specialist; see Chapter 11 for addresses.

Scindapsus

PRONUNCIATION: sin-DAP-suss
COMMON NAME: Pothos, devil's-ivy.
USES: Desktop, sill, hanging basket, pedestal.
LEAF COLOR: Green and gold.
FLOWERS: No.

Environmental Needs
LIGHT: Bright light but little or no direct sun; thrives in a fluorescent-light garden.
TEMPERATURE: 62–75°F.
HUMIDITY: Medium; tolerates much less.
MIST FREQUENTLY: Yes, if convenient.
SOIL MIX: All-purpose or African violet.
SOIL MOISTURE: Evenly moist to on the dry side.
PROPAGATION: Tip cuttings.
PROBLEMS: Nearly trouble-free. Severely dry soil will cause older leaves to turn yellow and die. Soggy wet, poorly drained soil will cause the roots and lower stems to rot.
COMMENTS: This plant is so common, it is often overlooked. However when well grown and displayed in a pretty basket or ceramic container, it can be truly beautiful.

Screw-pine: See **Pandanus**

Sea-grape: See **Coccoloba**

Sedum

> PRONUNCIATION: SEE-dum
> COMMON NAME: *S. morganianum* is the popular
> burro's-tail plant; there are many other sedums that
> make attractive house plants.
> USES: Desktop, sill, hanging basket, pedestal.
> LEAF COLOR: Green, blue-green, copper.
> FLOWERS: Pink, white, yellow.
>
> *Environmental Needs*
> LIGHT: Sunny east, south, or west window.
> TEMPERATURE: 62–72°F.
> HUMIDITY: Low.
> MIST FREQUENTLY: No.

Author

*Scindapsus, the common pothos, makes quite an uncommon
appearance when planted in an attractive bowl and given good
care.*

SOIL MIX: All-purpose.
SOIL MOISTURE: Evenly moist to on the dry side.
PROPAGATION: Tip or leaf cuttings.
PROBLEMS: Watch out for mealybugs. Avoid soggy wet, poorly drained soil which is likely to result in rooted roots and lower stems.
COMMENTS: Sedums are usually available from local shops, but for a wider selection, send away to mail-order specialists in cacti and other succulents; for addresses, see Chapter 11.

Setcreasea: See **Callisia**

Silver squill: See **Scilla**

Snake plant: See **Sansevieria**

Spathiphyllum

PRONUNCIATION: spath-uh-FILL-um
COMMON NAME: Peace lily.
USES: Desktop or sill if small; floor shrub or pedestal plant if large.
LEAF COLOR: Green.
FLOWERS: White.

Environmental Needs
LIGHT: Bright light, preferably near a sunny east, south, or west window, but placed so that little or no hot sun shines directly on the leaves.
TEMPERATURE: 62–75°F.
HUMIDITY: Medium; tolerates less.
MIST FREQUENTLY: Yes, if convenient.
SOIL MIX: All-purpose.
SOIL MOISTURE: Evenly moist to wet.
PROPAGATION: By division.
PROBLEMS: Severely dry soil causes the leaf tips to turn brown and die. Virtually pest-free.

This miniature sedum with coppery colored tips on blue-green leaves is only one of many that can be grown easily in a sunny window.

COMMENTS: One of the most durable and rewarding of all medium-size foliage plants with the added bonus of flowers off and on through the year. Some varieties grow only about 18 inches tall, others reach up to four feet.

Spider plant: See **Chlorophytum**

Staghorn fern: See **Platycerium**

Strelitzia

PRONUNCIATION: struh-LITZ-ee-uh
COMMON NAME: Bird-of-paradise.
USES: Floor shrub or pedestal.
LEAF COLOR: Blue-green.
FLOWERS: Orange and blue.
LIGHT: Sunny east, south, or west window.
TEMPERATURE: 60–70°F during the winter heating season.
HUMIDITY: Medium.
MIST FREQUENTLY: Yes, if convenient.
SOIL MIX: All-purpose.
SOIL MOISTURE: Evenly moist to on the dry side.
PROPAGATION: By division, but remember, strelitzia is more likely to flower if it fills the container with roots and leaves.
PROBLEMS: Red spider-mites may attack in air that is hot, dry, and stale; otherwise, strelitzia is trouble-free foliage plant, and if it flowers, you need feel no shame in proclaiming that you have two green thumbs.

Sultana: See **Impatiens**

Swedish ivy: See **Plectranthus**

Maddy Miller

Spathiphyllum is one of the best of all medium-size foliage plants, and in season it also sends up showy white flowers, as shown.

Sweet flag: See **Acorus**

Synadenium

PRONUNCIATION: sin-uh-DEEN-ee-um
COMMON NAME: Synadenium.
USES: Floor shrub.
LEAF COLOR: Green and burgundy.
FLOWERS: No.

Environmental Needs
LIGHT: Sunny, east, south, or west window.
TEMPERATURE: 62–75°F.
HUMIDITY: Low.
MIST FREQUENTLY: No.
SOIL MIX: All-purpose.
SOIL MOISTURE: Evenly moist to on the dry side.
PROPAGATION: Tip cuttings; allow cut end to dry in open air before planting.
PROBLEMS: Virtually none; a fail-safe foliage plant.
COMMENTS: Occasionally seen in local shops, especially among cacti and other succulents, even though synadenium is a leafy plant. Also available from mail-order specialists; see Chapter 11 for addresses.

Syngonium

PRONUNCIATION: sin-GOH-nee-um
COMMON NAME: Trileaf Wonder, nephthytis.
USES: Desktop, sill, hanging basket, pedestal.
LEAF COLOR: Green, chartreuse, silver.
FLOWERS: No.

Environmental Needs
LIGHT: Bright light but little or no direct sun shining on the leaves.

Trevesia is related to—and looks like common schefflera— but it is a better house plant, easy to grow.

TEMPERATURE: 62–75°F.
HUMIDITY: Medium; tolerates less.
MIST FREQUENTLY: Yes, if convenient.
SOIL MIX: All-purpose.
SOIL MOISTURE: Evenly moist.
PROPAGATION: Tip cuttings.
PROBLEMS: Mealybugs may attack, otherwise mostly pest-free.
COMMENTS: Young syngoniums grow as fairly compact bushes, but with age the stems need a totem pole on which to climb, or else you can train them to grow around and around a hanging basket.

Tahitian bridal veil: See Gibasis

Tangerine: See Citrus

Tolmiea

PRONUNCIATION: toll-MEE-uh
COMMON NAME: Piggyback or pickaback plant.
USES: Desktop, sill, hanging basket, pedestal.
LEAF COLOR: Green.
FLOWERS: No.

Environmental Needs
LIGHT: Bright but little or no hot sun shining directly on the leaves.
TEMPERATURE: 60–70°F during the winter heating season.
HUMIDITY: Medium; tolerates less.
MIST FREQUENTLY: Yes, if convenient.
SOIL MIX: All-purpose.
SOIL MOISTURE: Evenly moist.
PROPAGATION: Leaf cuttings.
PROBLEMS: Red spider-mites usually attack if the air is hot, dry, and stale. Severely dry soil causes old

leaves to turn brown and die. Avoid placement in drafts of hot air.

COMMENTS: Tolmiea is a relatively short-lived plant; it pays to start some leaf cuttings when the parent is 12–18 months old.

Tradescantia

PRONUNCIATION: tradd-ess-KANT-ee-uh
COMMON NAME: Wandering Jew.
USES: Hanging basket or pedestal.
LEAF COLOR: Green, white, purple, silver.
FLOWERS: Occasionally, but insignificant.

Environmental Needs
LIGHT: In or near a sunny east, south, or west window; insufficient light results in spindly, pale growth.
TEMPERATURE: 62–75°F.
HUMIDITY: Medium; tolerates less.
MIST FREQUENTLY: Yes, if convenient.
SOIL MIX: All-purpose.
SOIL MOISTURE: Evenly moist.
PROPAGATION: Tip cuttings.
PROBLEMS: Severely dry soil causes old leaves to die as well as the tips of younger ones. Roots and lower stems may rot if the soil is soggy wet and poorly drained for long periods of time. Frequent pinching back is necessary to encourage full, compact growth.
COMMENTS: Plain green tradescantias seem to tolerate low light better than the other kinds.

Trevesia

PRONUNCIATION: truh-VEE-zee-uh
COMMON NAME: Trevesia.
USES: Floor shrub or tree.

LEAF COLOR: Green.
FLOWERS: No.

Environmental Needs
LIGHT: Near a sunny east, south, or west window, but
sun shining directly on the leaves is not necessary.
TEMPERATURE: 62–75°F.
HUMIDITY: Medium.
MIST FREQUENTLY: Yes, if convenient.
SOIL MIX: All-purpose.
SOIL MOISTURE: Evenly moist.
PROPAGATION: Cuttings of half-mature stems.
PROBLEMS: Red spider-mites may attack in air that
is hot, dry, and stale; otherwise, trouble-free.
COMMENTS: This schefflera relative and look-alike is
much more easily cultivated; and hopefully will be-
come more generally available. In the meantime, it is
listed by Alberts & Merkel; see Chapter 11 for
address.

Trileaf Wonder: See **Syngonium**

Umbrella plant: See **Cyperus**

Unguentine plant: See **Aloe**

Vriesea

PRONUNCIATION: VREE-zee-uh
COMMON NAME: Vriesea, a bromeliad; flaming
sword.
USES: Desktop, sill, hanging basket, pedestal.
LEAF COLOR: Green, purple, red.
FLOWERS: Red, scarlet, yellow.

Environmental Needs
LIGHT: Sunny east, south, or west window; tolerates

257

Zingiber, whether the common plain-leaved form whose roots give us ginger, or this variegated green-and white variety, makes a good house plant.

Author

bright light without direct sun indefinitely if mature to begin with; thrives in a fluorescent-light garden.

TEMPERATURE: 62–75°F.

HUMIDITY: Medium to high; tolerates less.

MIST FREQUENTLY: Yes.

SOIL MIX: Cactus.

SOIL MOISTURE: Evenly moist to nearly dry; once a week, fill cup formed by leaves with clean water, but pour out old water before adding fresh.

PROPAGATION: By division, usually a few months after the plant has flowered.

PROBLEMS: None, unless roots stand in water for long periods of time, in which case the roots may rot.

COMMENTS: Many showy and unusual vrieseas are

available by mail from specialists; see Chapter 11 for addresses.

Wandering Jew: See **Tradescantia**

Watermelon begonia: See **Peperomia**

Waxplant: See **Hoya**

Zingiber

PRONUNCIATION: ZING-ib-er
COMMON NAME: Ginger.
USES: Sill, floor plant, or pedestal.
LEAF COLOR: Green or green and white.
FLOWERS: Yellow and purple.

Environmental Needs
LIGHT: Sunny east, south, or west window.
TEMPERATURE: 62–75°F.
HUMIDITY: Medium.
MIST FREQUENTLY: Yes, if convenient.
SOIL MIX: All-purpose.
SOIL MOISTURE: Evenly moist.
PROPAGATION: By division of the fleshy root.
PROBLEMS: Virtually trouble-free. Severely dry soil will cause the leaf tips to die back, but the root can survive long periods of dryness and resume growth when the soil is once again kept evenly moist.
COMMENTS: This is the ginger root used in cooking. You can grow your own ginger plant from a flat, firm piece of ginger root purchased from a green-grocer, and, in time, slice down into the pot and re-move a piece of fresh root for seasoning purposes.

11. By-Mail Sources for Never-Say-Die House Plants

Alberts & Merkel Bros., Inc., 2210 S. Federal Highway, Boynton Beach, Fla. 33435. Tropical foliage and flowering house plants, including orchids; send 25¢ for list.

John Brudy's Rare Plant House, P.O. Box 1348, Cocoa Beach, Fla. 32931. Unusual seeds and plants; $1 for catalog.

Buell's Greenhouses, Weeks Rd., Eastford, Conn. 06242. Complete listing of African violets, gloxinias and other gesneriads; $1 for catalog.

W. Atlee Burpee Co., 300 Park Ave., Warminster, Pa. 18974. Seeds and plants, plus supplies for growing house plants.

L. Easterbrook Greenhouses, 10 Craig St., Butler, Ohio 44822. African violets, other gesneriads, terrarium plants and supplies; $1 for catalog.

Henry Field Seed and Nursery Co., Shenandoah, Iowa 51601. House plants and supplies.

Fischer Greenhouses, Linwood, N.J. 08221. African violets and other gesneriads; supplies; 25¢ for catalog.

House Plant Corner, Ltd., Box 5000, Cambridge, Md. 21613. Supplies and equipment for growing house plants; 25¢ for catalog.

Hydroponic Chemical Co., Copley, Ohio 44321. Special fertilizers for house plants.

Kartuz Greenhouses, 92 Chestnut St., Wilmington, Mass. 01887. Begonias, gesneriads, house plants; one of the best by-mail sources for unusual plants; 50¢ for catalog.

Logee's Greenhouses, 55 North St., Danielson, Conn. 06239. Complete selection of common and unusual house plants; $1 for catalog.

Rod McLellan Co., 1450 El Camino Real, S. San Francisco, Calif. 94080. Orchids and supplies for growing them at home; makers of the nationally distributed soil-less growing medium called Supersoil.

Merry Gardens, Camden, Maine 04843. House plants and herbs; $1 for catalog.

George W. Park Seed Co., Inc., Greenwood, S.C. 29646. Seeds, bulbs, plants, fluorescent-light gardening equipment; large, complete catalog, free for the asking.

Stern's Nurseries, Geneva, N.Y. 14456. Makers of Stern's Mir-Acid fertilizer for acid-loving plants.

Sunnybrook Farms, 9448 Mayfield Rd., Chesterland, Ohio 44026. Herbs; wide assortment of house plants.

Three Springs Nurseries, Lilypons, Md. 21717. Aquarium plants.

Tinari Greenhouses, Box 190, 2325 Valley Rd., Huntingdon Valley, Pa. 19006. African violets, gesneriads, supplies and equipment; 25¢ for catalog.

Wilson Brothers, Roachdale, Ind. 47121. House plants.

SPECIALISTS IN CACTI/SUCCULENTS

Abbey Garden, 276 Toro Canyon Rd., Carpinteria, Calif. 93013. Complete listing of cacti and other succulents; 25¢ for catalog.

Fernwood Plants, 1311 Fernwood Pacific Dr., Topanga, Calif. 90290. Rare and unusual cacti.

Grigsby Cactus Gardens, 2354 Bella Vista Dr., Vista, Calif. 92083. 50¢ for catalog.

Henrietta's Nursery, 1345 N. Brawley Ave., Fresno, Calif. 93705. Cacti and other succulents; 20¢ for catalog.

Kirkpatrick's, 27785 De Anza St., Barstow, Calif. 92311. Cacti and other succulents; 10¢ for list.

SPECIALISTS IN ARTIFICIAL LIGHT FOR PLANTS

(*Note:* Ordinary and special agricultural fluorescents and incandescents, made by such firms as General Electric, Sylvania, Westinghouse, and Durotest are stocked by the firms listed here, except Verilux which sells only the Tru-Bloom. Many of the bulbs as well as fixtures are available at local electrical supply houses.)

Fleco Industries, 3347 Halifax St., Dallas, Tex. 75247. Attractive fluorescent-lighted shelves for plants.

Floralite Co., 4124 E. Oakwood Rd., Oak Creek, Wis. 53154. Fluorescent-light gardening equipment and supplies.

The Greenhouse, 9515 Flower St., Bellflower, Calif. 90706. Fluorescent-light gardening equipment.

Indoor Gardening Supplies, P.O. Box 40551, Detroit, Mich. 48240. Fluorescent-light gardening equipment.

J & D Lamps, 245 S. Broadway, Yonkers, N.Y. 10705. Fluorescent-light gardening equipment.

The Lite Factory, Ltd., 503 E. 72 St., New York, N.Y. 10021. Incandescent fixtures for growing plants.

Shoplite Co., Inc., 566 Franklin Ave., Nutley, N.J. 07110. Fluorescent-light gardening equipment; 25¢ for catalog.

Tube Craft, Inc., 1311 W. 80th St., Cleveland, Ohio 44102. Fluorescent-light gardening equipment.

Verilux TruBloom, 35 Mason St., Greenwich, Conn. 06830. Manufacturers of TruBloom fluorescents for plants.

SOURCES FOR POTTING SOIL

Excellent potting soils are generally available wherever house plants are sold. Many of the plant specialists listed earlier in this chapter also sell their own private label mixes. Newest on the market are the soil-less, peat-like, or synthetic growing mediums. If you have trouble finding a local source, contact any of the following:

Jiffy-Mix: George J. Ball, Inc., West Chicago, Ill. 60185.

Redi-Earth: W. R. Grace & Co., Construction Products Div., 62 Whittemore Ave., Cambridge, Mass. 02140.

Pro-Mix: Premier Peat Moss Corp., 25 W. 45th St., New York, N.Y. 10036.

Supersoil: Rod McLellan Co., 1450 El Camino Real, S. San Francisco, Calif. 94080.

Plant Pride: Organic Nutrients, Inc., 8909 Elder Creek Rd., Sacramento, Calif. 95828.

HELPFUL SOCIETIES AND PERIODICALS ABOUT HOUSE PLANTS

African Violet Magazine, bimonthly publication of the African Violet Society of America, Inc., Box 1326, Knoxville, Tenn. 37901.

American Fern Journal, quarterly publication of the American Fern Society, Biological Sciences Group, University of Connecticut, Storrs, Conn. 06268.

American Orchid Society Bulletin, monthly publication of the American Orchid Society, Inc., Botanical Museum of Harvard University, Cambridge, Mass. 02138.

The Begonian, monthly of the American Begonia Society, Inc., 139 N. Ledoux Rd., Beverly Hills, Calif. 90211.

The Bromeliad Journal, bimonthly publication of the Bromeliad Society, Inc., P.O. Box 3279, Santa Monica, Calif. 90403.

Epiphyllum Bulletin, publication of the Epiphyllum Society of America (Orchid Cacti), 218 E. Greystone Ave., Monrovia, Calif. 91016.

Monthly Fern Lessons, with newsletter and annual magazine, publications of the Los Angeles International Fern Society, 2423 Berritt Ave., Redondo Beach, Calif. 90278.

Gesneriad Saintpaulia News, bimonthly publication of Saintpaulia International and the American Gesneria Society, P.O. Box 10604, Knoxville, Tenn. 37919.

The Gloxinian, bimonthly publication of the American Gloxinia and Gesneriad Society, Inc., P.O. Box 174, New Milford, Conn. 06776.

Light Garden, bimonthly publication of the Indoor Light Gardening Society of America, Inc., 128 W. 58 St., New York, N.Y. 10019.

The Orchid Digest, 25 Ash Ave., Corte Madera, Calif. 94925.

Plants Alive, monthly magazine about indoor gardening, 1255 Portland Place, Boulder, Colo. 80302.

Popular Gardening Indoors, periodical about indoor gardening, 383 Madison Avenue, New York, N.Y. 10017.

Principes, quarterly publication of the Palm Society, 1320 S. Venetian Way, Miami, Fla. 33139.

Terrarium Topics, published by the Terrarium Association, 57 Wolfpit Ave., Norwalk, Conn. 06851.

12. How to Be an Electric Gardener

If the windows of your house or apartment don't receive enough sun for the plants you want to grow, or if you want to grow plants in interior spaces which receive no direct sun, artificial light can be the answer. Fluorescent is far more efficient than incandescent, but each has its place in the rapidly expanding world of electric gardening. Either fluorescent or incandescent lamps may be used to supplement natural light, but if artificial light is the sole source of illumination, fluorescent is far superior. In fact, most authorities question the feasibility of using incandescents presently available as the sole source of light for growing plants.

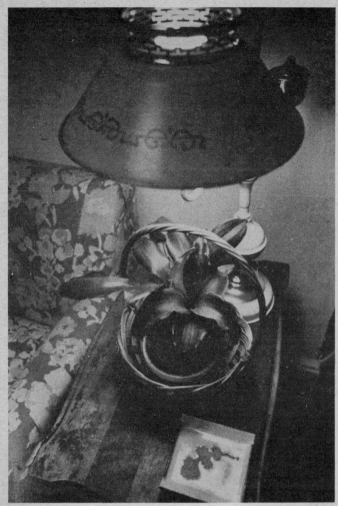

Author

Bird's-nest sansevieria is one of the few plants that will grow well indefinitely in the light cast by an ordinary table lamp burned approximately ten hours daily or more, with no supplementary natural light.

Author

This tabletop garden, seen through the leaves of an indoor avocado tree, receives pale natural light through the daytime, but thrives with supplementary light received every evening from the tablelamp. Oxalis regnellii *and wax begonias bloom here most of the year.*

The simplest way you can use artificial light for plants is to use an ordinary table lamp to supplement natural light. As a supplement to weak natural light, a 60- to 150-watt bulb burned six to eight hours each evening can do wonders for practically any plant small enough to fit comfortably under the edge of the shade within the range of maximum light. If you have a windowless office at work, with ceiling fluorescents burned 8–10 hours daily, and a reading lamp with one or two incandescents, plants will do surprisingly well clustered around the lamp on your desk.

Incandescent floods with built-in reflectors (General Electric's Cool Beam, Sylvania's Cool Lux, Duro-Lite's Plant Lite), available generally in sizes from 75 to 150 watts, are excellent for growing and maintaining large

This adjustable floor lamp with a 40-watt bulb is used more to dramatize the beauty of the grape-ivy (cissus) at night than to supplement .natural light. If the artificial light were required to sustain growth, a 75- to 150-watt floodlight would be needed, and it would have to be at least two feet away from the foliage to avoid burning.

Bill Mulligan

foliage plants, indoor trees, hanging baskets and collections of smaller plants. These are·to be used only in fixtures with ceramic sockets, and take care not to splash water on them while they are lighted. Wattage needed will vary, depending on the size and kind of plant, and whether or

Bill Mulligan

These adjustable floodlights give supplementary light, and help create dramatic effects.

271

Bill Mulligan; Designer Del Blessinger

An uplight makes this ficus tree look its best at night, but light coming from below leaves has little effect other than cosmetic.

not it receives any natural light, or long and daily doses of light from ceiling fluorescents as in an office building. The same holds true of how long the flood needs to be burned daily. For a true low-light plant or one receiving some natural light, six hours illumination each evening may be sufficient. For plants that need more light or those that receive no natural light, burning the flood 16 hours out of every 24 may be required. A 75-watt incandescent flood may be placed as close as 24 inches from the leaves without any danger of overheating them. Larger floods may need to be placed as much as three feet away from the leaves. The general rule is to be sure the flood isn't so close that it makes the leaves feel warm or hot to the touch of your fingers. Be especially careful with thin-textured, delicate leaves such as ferns and begonias when using supplementary incandescent light.

One of the greatest advantages to using incandescent floods for growing plants, whether they are the sole or merely a supplementary light source, is that their effect can be flattering and dramatic, and at the same time they are utilitarian and beneficial. Depending on the fixtures used, the lighting can be down, up, or across. Experiment at night, moving the flood or floods variously to play up flowers, foliage, or shadows on the wall or ceiling. Re-

Author

An easy way to provide ideal light for an indoor garden measuring two feet wide and four feet long is to suspend a fluorescent unit with two 40-watt tubes over the table or other surface on which plants will be placed.

273

This prefabricated unit by Fleco Industries for growing plants with artificial light comes equipped with three sets of two 20-watt fluorescents. Here it is used primarily for growing a collection of bromeliads and sansevierias.

Author

member, however, that for the best growth response, the light should come from above or to the side of the plant; uplights tend to flatter plants the same way footlights flatter people, but plants are conditioned to give the best growth response to light received from above, not from below.

Uplights for dramatic lighting of plants are best equipped with PAR bulbs, special floods that focus a narrower and stronger beam of light than conventional floods. The result is less glare in your eyes and more light to flatter your plants. These bulbs are available from many manufacturers and may be used in any standard floor cannister fixture.

For lighting a fairly large plant from the side or above, a relatively inexpensive, adjustable photographer's light stand may be used, equipped with a ceramic socket. Adjustable-arm-type fixtures, such as architect's drafting-table lamps also offer great flexibility of movement without your having to move the whole fixture. They can offer supplementary light to a number of plants and still be kept on the desk or tabletop where they're used for reading.

Track lighting is becoming increasingly popular among interior designers and people who want interesting yet unobtrusive lighting effects in their rooms. These systems offer, without a doubt, the most versatile room lighting available. And a single track light equipped with a flood is perfect for promoting new growth at the top of a tall plant where sunlight from windows seldom reaches.

Small adjustable-arm lamps of the Tensor type are ideal for dramatizing the colorful blooms of small flowering plants, such as African violets, gloxinias, and miniature roses. The colors of these may be lost in a large room but become brilliant attention getters when spotlighted with a Tensor-type lamp. Be careful not to place the light too close to the plants, however, or delicate leaves and petals may be burned. It is doubtful that the light given off by one of these is of much benefit to the plant, but it does help you and your friends enjoy it more.

FLUORESCENT-LIGHT GARDENING. A basic fluorescent-light setup for plants is pure simplicity. All you need is a fixture with two 20-watt or two 40-watt tubes suspended approximately 18 inches above a table, bench, or shelf on which the flowerpots and other containers will rest. Burn the lights 14–16 hours out of every 24. Uniform day length is important, and for this reason I recommend the use of an automatic timer.

The easiest way to become a fluorescent-light gardener is to buy a fixture designed and prefabricated for the purpose. By-mail sources for these are listed in Chapter 11. Some available are purely utilitarian, others are decorative as well as functional. The main thing to avoid is any plant light unit that comes equipped with less than 40 watts of illumination.

There are many different kinds of fluorescents on the market. I have had excellent results for many years by using a combination of one Cool White with one Warm White in each fixture. More recently I have been using a combination of one Cool White with any one of the broad-spectrum horticultural lamps such as Agro-Lite, Natur-Escent, Verilux Tru-Bloom, Vita-Lite and Wide-Spectrum

Bill Mulligan

This more utiliatarian prefabricated unit by Tube Craft, Inc., for growing plants provides 24 square feet of tray space, but requires a floor area that measures only two feet by four feet. The owner of this one drapes plastic over it at night to increase humidity around the African violets.

The space between kitchen cabinets and spare countertop has been used her for nurturing an impressive collection of bromeliads by installing a fixture with two 40-watt fluorescent tubes in it.

Gro-Lux. Under no circumstance do I recommend the use of incandescents in the same fixture with fluorescents. They give off excessive heat, burn less efficiently, and as far as I can tell do more damage by drying out the air than they benefit the plants.

Some of the mail-order firms listed in Chapter 11, as well as local electrical supply houses stock the components to build your own setups above a bookcase, over a kitchen counter, or concealed behind a valance over a sunless window, for example. For maximum light reflection in a bookcase or similar situation, coat the back wall and two end surfaces with flat white paint. Or, for reflection and dramatic effect, mirror these surfaces, either with pieces of pre-cut, self-sticking mirror tile or peel-and-stick Mylar.

With present-day equipment, the limitation of fluorescent-light gardens is that the tubes must be within a few inches of the plants. Kinds that grow fairly low and compact are the best. When you consider the large number of plants which fit these requirements, the limitations seem hardly worth considering. For example, in my apartment I have two fluorescent-light gardens which give a total of 30 square feet of growing space. Some of the plants growing well include African violets, miniature gloxinias, an orchid called *Diacrium bicornutum* which flowers several months each year, many different ferns, oxalis, a collection of naturally small bromeliads, coleus, fittonia, maranta, episcia, peperomia, philodendron, hoya and calathea, to name just a few.

13. How to Make Your Plants Beautiful

If beauty lies in the eye of the beholder, then you may look at your dracaena with dead leaf tips and see only a beautiful corn plant that is actually contributing its share of green to your apartment. Or the leafy branches of your ficus tree may help you ignore the dead leaves it has dropped all around. But if you want to gain the reputation among your friends for having a supergreen thumb, you'll want to make your plants look as though they live in a constant state of glamorous well-being.

Keeping plants well-groomed and attractively displayed is part of what makes gardening indoors an endless source of pleasure. And, if you keep the leaves clean by showering them every few weeks or months with tepid water, the plants will not only look better, but they probably will be healthier. Plants small enough to be carried easily may be rinsed off in the kitchen or bathroom sink. Ask a friend to help you carry larger plants to the bathtub. And if moving the plant is unthinkable, sprinkle the leaves generously with your mister. If it's physically possible, move your plants outdoors (but not African violets) during a gentle, warm (outdoor temperatures should be 60 degrees or more) rain.

Keeping dead leaves and withered flowers trimmed off plants makes them look better, but also reduces the likelihood of disease or insect problems. If the tip or edge of a leaf has turned yellow or brown, you can trim off only the dead part, using a pair of scissors and cutting just enough

Bill Mulligan

Placing plants in attractive baskets, or elevating a special one, helps make them more beautiful. Here they are (from left to right) a cereus cactus, a Norfolk Island pine (araucaria) and a prayer plant (maranta).

Maddy Miller

Grouping plants of a kind (not necessarily the same variety) fosters the collector spirit. Here four different kinds of agla-onema or Chinese evergreen or displayed in pedestals and pots of various heights but complimentary colors.

281

A few plants well grown and thoughtfully displayed can have a more pleasing effect than a jungle tangle of poorly groomed plants. The fronds of a kentia palm frame the photograph; others, from left to right, include Dracaena fragrans, *Boston fern, star begonia, with another Boston fern hanging, along with wandering Jew (tradescantia) and Tahitian bridal veil (gibasis).*

Steps of any kind make an excellent place to display house plants; from the top, these are aucuba or golddust plant (treat as ficus), coleus and schefflera.

of the green to give the leaf a natural shape. A big palm with lots of fronds lined with dead leaf tips can keep you busy and satisfy your tactile senses for a couple of hours, especially if also you bathe or wipe each leaf between two pieces of moist paper toweling.

A plant tree like this one is an excellent way to show off and grow potted plants in a traditional setting. The plants are, from the top, peperomia, scindapsus, peperomia, 'Fluffy Ruffles' fern, Boston fern, English ivy and gynura (purple passion; treat as plectranthus).

One sure way to make a plant look special is to place its pot inside a slightly larger, decorative container. I use baskets, handcrafted pottery, and polished chrome cylinders. If water would harm the decorative container you wish to use, a basket for example, be sure the saucer you place under the plant pot is waterproof and deep enough to avoid spillovers. (Unglazed clay pot saucers allow some moisture to seep through; place a piece of cork under saucers of this type.) Depending on the appearance of the plant and its decorative container, a ground cover of florists' sheet moss or pebbles may make the perfect finishing touch.

Avenir

Matching pedestals and plant containers like these are available in a wide range of prices, and in various sizes and finishes. The cylinders shown are sheathed in split bamboo and come in heights varying from six to 48 inches.

Pieces of Featherock with planting pockets carved out make naturally beautiful containers for cacti and other succulents. not to mention almost any plant of a size suited to that of the rock. African violets in particular grow well in Featherock.

One of my favorite ways to display my plants is to place them on pedestals and platforms of various heights. If you have lots of different kinds of plants, this staging technique can be used to make certain specimens stand out, especially at a time when they are unusually beautiful.

A pedestal can be anything from clean clay pots turned upside down and stacked at various levels, found concrete electrical conduit, medium-priced shiny Mylar- or grass-cloth-covered cylinders to expensive, custommade pedestals or platforms of Plexiglas, Lucite, or wood. Useful heights include 12, 18, 24, 36, and 48 inches; diameters can vary from 8 to 10 inches for a 12- to 18-inch height, to 12 inches or more for any height; platforms may be of any size from 12-inch cubes up, depending on the space and environment you have in mind.

Inexpensive wooden stepladders painted to match the room in which they are used also make a great place to display plants, some with dangling stems, others with contrasting upright growth.

You'll be more successful as an indoor gardener if you limit the number of plants to kinds suited to the environment you can provide. Think also about the amount of time you can spend, for each plant does in fact require a long-term commitment on your part. I would rather see five plants well-grown and beautifully displayed, with sensitivity both to appearance and environmental needs, than 50 poorly-groomed plants growing in a jungle tangle.

Green Thumb Answers To House Plant Questions

Everything the indoor gardener needs to know about house plants, with easy-to-follow instructions for their care, problems and propagation